Bishop Francis Hodur

SERMON OUTLINES
AND
OCCASIONAL SPEECHES
1899 - 1922

Bishop Francis Hodur

SERMON OUTLINES
AND
OCCASIONAL SPEECHES
1899 - 1922

Translated and Edited
by
Theodore L. Zawistowski

General Editor
Casimir J. Grotnik

SCRANTON, PENNSYLVANIA

CENTRAL DIOCESE
POLISH NATIONAL CATHOLIC CHURCH

EAST EUROPEAN MONOGRAPHS, BOULDER
DISTRIBUTED BY COLUMBIA UNIVERSITY PRESS, NEW YORK

1999

Library of Congress Catalog Card Number 99-70481

ISBN 0-944497-13-6

Printed through the courtesy of the
Paul and Carrie Griglak Fund
Central Diocese
Polish National Catholic Church

TABLE OF CONTENTS

SEASONAL SERMONS

FOREWORD

In the course of his work as the archivist of the Central Diocese of the Polish National Catholic Church of America, Father Senior Casimir J. Grotnik discovered a few notebooks with notes written in the hand of Bishop Franciszek Hodur. These were outlines for sermons and occasional speeches spanning the years from 1899 to 1922. These notes are of special interest to members of the Polish National Catholic Church on various topics, including original sin, devotion of Mary, the labor movement, eternal life, reasons for the organization of the Church, the aspirations of Polish people regarding their homeland, and many other topics.

Father Tadeusz Kluzek transcribed these handwritten notes to typewritten form. Father Senior Grotnik then set the type, making it possible to publish these notes in the original Polish and a limited number of copies were printed.

I am especially grateful to Father Doctor Grotnik and to Father Kluzek for their labor in preparing the material for printing and distribution. My sincere thanks to them. I also thank Theodore L. Zawistowski for translating these materials and annotating them.

It is my prayer that this work will increase our understanding of the work of Bishop Hodur and those who together with him gave life and direction to the work to which they were called by God.

Anthony M. Rysz

Bishop, Central Diocese
Polish National Catholic Church

GENERAL EDITOR'S FOREWORD

Bishop Francis Hodur (1866-1953), the organizer of the Polish National Catholic Church in America and in Poland, was a charismatic preacher and speaker.

According to his contemporaries, those persons who heard him listened with bated breath, sometimes for a number of hours.

We have many sermons and addresses by Bishop Hodur from such sources as *Straż* [The Guard] and *Rola Boża* [God's Field] as well as the notes of Savonarola Theological Seminary students and priests.

The sermon outlines and occasional speeches which we present in this collection were taken from original manuscripts of Bishop Hodur that had not been published previously. They are found in the collections of the Bishop Hodur Biography Commission. In many instances they were dated in the original.

These handwritten notes were deciphered by Father Tadeusz Kluzek. He and Father Edward Czudak corrected the final copy, for which I am very grateful to them.

Casimir J. Grotnik

General Editor and
Central Diocese Archivist

INTRODUCTION

The materials in this volume come from a collection of handwritten sermon outlines and occasional speeches contained in a small number of notebooks, some in pieces, preserved from the beginning of the twentieth century. Clearly, they were ideas jotted down by their author, Father, and later, Bishop Francis Hodur, for his own use, often hastily scrawled in ink, pencil or even colored pencil, with occasional additions, corrections or marginal notes scattered throughout, including, in one instance, a little drawing. When reading these materials, it should be remembered that in those days sermons lasting half an hour were common and hour-long sermons were not unusual. Therefore, one should not be too quick to conclude that what was written is all that was said.

There are in existence a few recordings of Bishop Hodur speaking publicly as well as some silent films and photographs. Using his deep, well-modulated voice, his style of address could range from the calm, thoughtful and serious to fiery anger punctuated with dramatic gestures, varying with the audience and the occasion. He was never known to read a sermon, always seeming to speak extemporaneously. His notes show that he often, perhaps usually, collected his thoughts beforehand.

Generations of students at Savonarola Theological Seminary preparing for the priesthood in the Polish National Catholic Church were required to take notes of Bishop Hodur's sermons for later review and discussion. After ordination, when they tried to read his sermons in their own parishes, many found that just reading his words aloud did not get the same effect in the congregations that he did with his powerful delivery.

The collection represented in this volume came from the estate of Father Marian Czerny and was donated to the Bishop Hodur Biography Commission of the Central Diocese of the Polish National Catholic Church by his widow, Sophia, in 1975.

Father Tadeusz Kluzek transcribed most, but not all, of the materials in the collection, which were then prepared for publication by Father Senior Casimir J. Grotnik. The translations in this booklet, therefore, are not from the original manuscripts but from that publication, *Szkice do kazań i przemówień 1899 –1921* [Outlines of Sermons and Speeches 1899 – 1921], published in 1998 in Scranton, Pennsylvania, by the Central Diocese. However, in the process of preparing the present publication, it was decided to rearrange the order of presentation, make annotations, and add three pieces: "Sacrament of Confirmation" and the introductions to the Special General Synod of the Polish National Catholic Church held in Scranton in 1906.

"Sacrament of Confirmation" is a unique piece in this collection because it is the only one authored by him in English and provides a rare example in a composition written in his own hand of Bishop Hodur's ability to use the language.

A much larger and more complete collection of sermons or homilies by Bishop Hodur, prepared by Father Grotnik, was published in 1977 by the Bishop Hodur Biography Commission under the title *Kazania Biskupa Hodura* [Sermons of Bishop Hodur]. Covering the entire liturgical year, it was based primarily on published sources, especially *Rola Boża* [God's Field], the official publication of the Polish National Catholic Church. However, since that book has not yet been translated, the present collection can serve as both an additional sample of Bishop Hodur's homiletic style and as an introduction to it in English for those who do not read Polish.

The growing body of work in English pertaining to Bishop Hodur also allows one to begin to gain a better grasp of his many-sided complexity. It might prove fruitful, for example, to compare the present texts with those in my *Hodur: A Compilation of Selected Translations* (1990) and in Joseph W. Wieczerzak, *Bishop Francis Hodur: Biographical Essays* (1998).

In addition to the ordinary religious and moral topics to be expected in the sermons of a parish pastor, Bishop Hodur's themes also include his views on theological problems, denominational challenges, social justice, ethnic issues, political questions, patriotic subjects, historical events, and more.

Bible students might notice that Bishop Hodur's citations may not always conform to some of the more familiar versions of the Scripture. This is due in part to his reliance on the 1599 Polish translation by Father Jakub Wujek of the Latin Vulgate. Considering that these notes were to himself and not prepared for publication, he may have written some citations from memory as he was writing. Some citations in the notes are incomplete, for example, giving chapter but not verse, or no reference at all. This may also explain the occasional use of an alternate term. On the other hand, since he was trained as a Roman Catholic priest, he may have known the familiar citations in Latin as well as in Polish. He is acknowledged to have had an excellent grasp of Latin. He also studied Greek for several years. Therefore his occasional turn of a Biblical phrase herein may or may not have been intended. He also liked to put two or three separated verses together in a single line, which can be made visible on the printed page but that may or may not sound distinctly separate when spoken.

As to the translation from Polish to English, one can only hope that there are not too many questionable instances. The translations from Scripture here are taken from the New American Catholic Edition (1954) except where Bishop Hodur may have used an alternative term.

Perhaps the single most obvious quibble has to do with the Polish word *człowiek,* which can be used for an individual *man* or the collective *Man.* In this our day of gender sensitivity, it was decided to use variations such as *person* or *humankind* to avoid what some might feel to be sexist terminology. Of course, ninety or a hundred years ago a single gender term was not regarded as sexist. But that is one of the problems to be expected when translating not only from one language to another but also from one historical period to another.

A few words of appreciation are hereby expressed to Joseph W. Wieczerzak for his assistance in various aspects of this undertaking and also to Father Doctor Grotnik.

Biographical and Historical Note

Born in the village of Żarki in 1866 in southwestern Poland not far from the ancient capital city of Cracow, near to what was to become during World War II the infamous death camp of Auschwitz, and close to the town where Pope John Paul II was born, Franciszek [Francis] Hodur was educated at the Jagiellonian University and its affiliated school of theology. In 1893, he came to the United States and was soon ordained a Roman Catholic priest in Scranton, where he became an assistant pastor at Sacred Hearts of Jesus and Mary Church. Not long after, he was named pastor of Holy Trinity Church in nearby Nanticoke, but then made the momentous step in 1897 of accepting a call to lead the dissidents breaking away from Sacred Hearts of Jesus and Mary Parish. Events subsequently unfolded leading to the formation of the Polish National Catholic Church of America, which held its First Synod in 1904 and elected him bishop. He was consecrated a bishop by the Old Catholic Archbishop of Utrecht in 1907. Bishop Hodur served as the head of the new religious denomination until his death in 1953, leaving a legacy which has endured to this day not only in the United States but also in Poland and Canada.

The materials in this volume therefore touch upon the formative years of the Polish National Catholic Church in the United States when immigrants from subjugated Poland were flowing to America in huge numbers and encountering an unfamiliar American version of their traditional Roman Catholic Church, followed by the upheaval of World War I and the liberation of Poland.

Theodore L. Zawistowski

Sacrament of Confirmation[1]

(This is not a translation. It was written in Bishop Hodur's own handwriting in a booklet containing other of his outlines in Polish. The brackets, however, are the editor's.)

Then they laid their hands on them and they received the Holy Spirit.
Acts 8:17

I am very glad to see you again, my Brethren and Sisters, and am very satisfied that I was able to come to you and confer upon your children the sacrament of confirmation. Through this sacrament the Holy Ghost imparted to the confirmed the gifts and graces to make them perfect Christians and gives them strength and courage to confess openly the Christian and Catholic faith. Confirmation is the perfection, the plenitude and consummation of the grace of baptism; this is to say, it confirms, augments and perfects the grace which it finds already existing in him on whom it is conferred. You received, my children, through this sacrament the gifts of the Holy Spirit, that you may be better (that you may grow) stronger in the service to God and men. You received the gift of wisdom, which makes you love the goods of eternity and removes you from everything opposed to our Lord, and the gift of understanding, which makes you comprehend the truths of Christian religion; the gift of counsel, which makes you choose whatever will contribute most to the glory of God and our salvation; the gift of fortitude, which gives you courage to profess our religion openly, to overcome temptations, to resist even at the peril of our lives, the fury of persecution; the gift of knowledge, which makes you know the will of God in whatever concerns your salvation and discovers to you the dangers which you must avoid; the gift of piety, which unites you with God in a particular manner

---

[1] June 28, 1914. This sermon may have been delivered to the independent Italian Parish of St. Anthony of Padua in Passaic, New Jersey, when some 1000 persons received the Sacrament of Confirmation. At one time some 26 Italian parishes were associated with the Polish National Catholic Church.

11

and in fine [?] the gift of fear, which inspires you with respect for God and makes you shun whatever is contrary to his holy will. You have received also today all graces and gifts from God in this holy sacrament of confirmation; be therefore grateful to God, correspond with His favors, be true to your promises and resolutions that you ma[y] be good workers and soldiers for eternal salvation. Never be ashamed of the Gospel of J. Ch., never be ashamed of your parochial church, of your religion. Conform your lives to the holy live of our Savior J. Chr. — your divine model; walk in the footsteps of the Apostles and the primitive Christians in the path of virtue and you will obtain the crown of immortality promised to those who [shall?] shall have fought the good fight of the Lord to the end.

Amen.

OCCASIONAL SERMONS AND SPEECHES

Poland at the Border of Two Centuries[2]

Soon the clock of time will ring the last hour of the nineteenth century and will begin to peal the first moments of the new century. And the most simple folk and the most deeply learned are giving to this change of time at least a little attention. What will this new age bring to humankind, what paths will it take, will humanity attain that so desired happiness, or, as in past ages, will it struggle with poverty of soul and body and after a hundred years of effort find itself at the gates of the twenty-first century like Sisyphus pushing the stone up the hill only, after it falls down, to again push it up the hill? It is clear that no one mortal can answer this question definitely. Truly the world and all humankind develop according to eternal laws but also that in the unknown rules of these laws there is a mystery.

History shows us such past epochs in which humankind stood high in culture, built splendid cities such as Babylon and Rome, and created well-organized states: Ramses three thousand years ago on the Nile, Caesar Augustus in the time of Christ. And then the cities and the states decayed and their civilizations turned into wrecks. In their place came new races and people who trampled the old and splendid cultures, and began again from ABC.

Therefore, cannot the same happen with today's people of the white Latin-Germanic race what has already been repeated several times? Why not?

However, for the moment let our heads not ache over the whole of human society. We will think only about Poland as we stand at the brink of the nineteenth and twentieth centuries.

What will happen with our nation in the future age? Will we die devoured by the Germans or the Muscovites? Or will we be capable of self existence? That is the question! "To be or not to

---

[2] 1899-1900.

13

be" bursts forth from the lips of Poland, that Hamlet among nations at the end of the nineteenth and the beginning of the twentieth centuries, and the world replies to this question in various ways.

Those of the Prussian and Russian type of henchmen claim that they will swallow us, that we will not last to the next century. Others again, and there are more of them, foresee a long life for us, if only we ourselves do not think of death. And who would think about his demise?

The end of the past century found us completely not prepared for the struggle for survival. The much smaller Prussian statelet so managed to guide European politics that the Polish Republic was dismantled without hue and cry because there were not enough capable politicians who could countervail the plans of Frederick II, or enough armies to defend the borders of the Polish state.[3]

Our nation found itself at the precipice but did not want to save itself. The exhortations of Stanisław Leszczyński, Konarski, Staszic, brought only relative benefit.[4] They did not awaken the majority of that nation which did not see in the discord of the nobility a political ideal.

Even that terrible cruelty which befell Poland in the year 1772 did not shake her organism to the core in order for a change for the better to occur.[5] As in the times of the Saxon kings and Poniatowski, so in the times of the partition of Poland our nobility gathered, gobbled and expected that somehow things will be.[6] The whole nation did not have an awareness of its great misfortune, just some individuals, and therefore it did not achieve regeneration. In

---

[3]The Polish-Lithuanian Commonwealth was partitioned in 1792 and 1795 by Prussia, Russia and Austria.

[4]Stanisław I Leszczyński (1677-1766), twice King of Poland, later Duke of Lorraine and Bar. Both Stanisław Konarski (1700-1773) and Stanisław Staszyc (or Staszic) (1755-1826) were leading social, economic and political reformers.

[5]In 1772, the first partition of Poland occurred when its eastern territories were seized by the Russian Empire.

[6]Augustus II Wettin (1670-1733), King of Poland and Elector of Saxony; Augustus III Wettin (1696-1763), King of Poland and Elector of Saxony; Stanisław August Poniatowski (1732-1798), the last King of Poland. For over two hundred years, the Kings of the Polish-Lithuanian Commonwealth were elected to office.

truth, the great troublemaking plans of Napoleon shook Poland, but only superficially. The nation dozed, and bowed once to Napoleon and then again to his defeaters.

The fact that exactly at the time of the partitions and after the partitions of Poland our nobility obtained the most princely titles and medals from the royal courts inimical to us sadly testifies to the patriotism of the upper classes of our nation.

"The baboon of nations and parrot" Słowacki called the Poland of that time, and he did not sin greatly, for the nation instead of gathering itself, determining its state of affairs and energetically getting to work, Poles looked to other nations and aped Paris or Vienna.

In truth in each generation are to be found some leaders burning with fervent love for the Fatherland, but they do not know how to infuse their beliefs into the nation, or by their wishful, utopian ideas lead society into new wildernesses.

Even such great minds as Mickiewicz, Słowacki and Krasiński[7] delayed in some respects the healing of the nation, talking it into martyrdom and the foreordaining of Poland by Providence for the liberation of humankind from its fall. They called Poland the messiah of nations. They only forgot that Christ suffered for others' sins while the Poles for their own thoughtlessness, wastefulness, disharmony, and stupidity.

Only the year 1863 brought a warning and a better understanding of the directions we are to take, which are required to improve conditions and to achieve a better situation.[8]

The year 1863 our great friend Brandes called "an epoch in the spiritual life of Poland."[9] And rightly so, because the adolescent thoughtlessness, the traditional gullibility, that France or England

---

[7]Adam Mickiewicz (1798-1855), Juliusz Słowacki (1809-1849) and Zygmunt Krasiński (1812-1859) were three of Poland's greatest poets. The figures of Mickiewicz and Słowacki appear in stained glass windows in St. Stanislaus Bishop and Martyr Cathedral Polish National Catholic Church in Scranton, Pennsylvania.

[8]In 1863 the January Insurrection attempted but failed to expel the Russians from the part of Poland they occupied.

[9]Brandes, p. 49.

are only waiting to save us from slavery, and that childish disrespect for the brutal force of the enemy, were replaced with cold assessment.

In the place of yearnings and romantic pictures, naked Polish reality presents itself before each one and speaks more or less as follows: "Your situation in Poland is worthy of regret but it is not pitiable. You have lost much but not everything, because the foundation is untouched. You have many healthy and inborn talents, therefore awaken yourself from lethargy. To work!

> *Hey to work, together to work . . .*
> *We beggars, therefore kinsmen,*
> *work today is our weapon!*

These healthy slogans spread over the expanses of the old Polish Republic and called forth on faces not long before gray and pale the blush of health and life.

As if at the touch of magic wands, life transforms, boils and surges in every domain, if, however, not so splendidly and strong as in France, England or the United States, yet it testifies that we are not some tribe condemned to death but a healthy, strong and immortal nation.

All the results of human work have their representation among us. Previously nonexistent commerce and trade, admittedly with the help of foreign capital, are erecting factories in Łódź, Warsaw, Częstochowa, Pabanice, Poznań . . . and is now beginning to stir in Galicia.[10] Literature and fine arts are producing people such as Kraszewski, Sienkiewicz, Prus, Miłkowski, Orzeszkowa, Matejko, Grottger, Siemiradzki, Chopin, and Moniuszko.[11]

---

[10]Galicia was the name given to the southern part of Poland that was occupied by the Austro-Hungarian Empire. The large industrial cities named here were in the areas of Poland occupied by the German or Russian Empires.

[11]Józef Ignacy Kraszewski (1812-1887), poet; Henryk Sienkiewicz (1846-1916), author; Bolesław Prus (Aleksander Głowacki) (1847-1912), author; Zygmunt Miłkowski (T. T. Jeż) (1824-1915), author; Eliza Orzeszkowa (1841-1910), author; Jan Matejko (1838-1893), artist; Artur Grottger (1837-1867), artist; Henryk Siemiradzki (1843-1902),

Our musicians and actors are winning applause in Paris, London and New York, and scholars and inventors of such stature as Olszewski and Szczepanik have been listed among the leaders who are pushing the earthly globe forward.[12]

We have no cause therefore to be ashamed that we are Poles. Indeed, we should be proud that we are subjugated and yet we do not walk with our heads like slaves living from the crumbs of our masters but that despite difficult conditions of life we live our own lives.

The providence of God will give us an opportunity to serve once again universal and global purposes. Napoleon used to say that if an awakened nation wishes to achieve some goal with all the force of its will, sooner or later it will win the object of its desires. Therefore may our whole nation awaken itself, may it desire independent life and may it exert its will and strength, and we will have a Polish state in the twentieth century.

Religion[13]

I did not come here to impose my views on those listening but to present a certain subject and shed some light on it. And if this should bring you a little help and benefit, I shall be greatly pleased.

The subject of my reflections is religion, religion in the broadest sense of the term, as a characteristic of the human being seeking union with the highest being, with God Himself. I chose this subject because as a priest I am more closely tied to this aspect of human tendencies and also because I wish to bring to my countrymen's attention manifestations of human life. Among us

---

artist; Frederic (Fryderyk) Chopin (1810-1849), composer; Stanisław Moniuszko (1819-1872), composer.

[12]Karol Olszewski (1846-1915), first liquified oxygen and nitrogen; Jan Szczepanik (1872-1926), called "the Polish Edison."

[13][1925?]. The booklet in which this item was found clearly was used for very different purposes over widely separated times.

Poles religion has been either a forgotten field or the cause of our political, social and spiritual enslavement.

It is a certain thing that for half a century weak religious inclinations have dominated the present generation. The assertion that since humankind has had its history none of the needs and desires which it has manifested have disappeared, and that religions have played in the world such a great role that it is appropriate to regard them as deeply rooted in human nature.

Of a similar conclusion is the Swiss thinker Georges Sorel, who in his book *Religion in Today's World* writes as follows:[14]

> For a long time philosophers were convinced that a conflict exists between science and religion which should continue to grow in meaning and since they could not accept that the modern world would reject science asked themselves by what means to arrive at a replacement for religion. Particularly numerous were philanthropic inventions which had as a purpose the organization of sacrifice for others. Today the situation has changed because in general we do not see now a reason why science and religion cannot develop peacefully.

In Polish society such voices are practically unknown because, as I observed earlier, hardly anyone thinks about religion as a creative force, as a worldview, from which springs joy, relief and happiness. From this point of view, looking at the Polish nation we must admit the reasoning of the author of *Wartości twórcze religijnej myśli polskiej* [The Creative Values of Polish Religious Thought] where on page 112 she expresses herself thus:

> Today's Poland is a country deprived of religious thought. In none of the European societies, except perhaps with the exceptions of Spain and Portugal, religious questions are not in general something so foreign, something such a meaningless addition for consideration. In truth, among us even too many phrases are pronounced about the attachment of the nation to the faith of the father and so forth, but in reality this supposed attachment is only a screen for the essential irreligiousness of the average modern Pole. People without religion are as likely among the average members of the

---

[14]Georges Sorel (1847-1922) was an early Swiss sociologist.

dominant Catholic Church as among its average opponents. They do not comprehend that religion is something that constitutes the internal, guiding relationship of a person to all of his personal feelings, desires, actions, and intentions, and about his active external relationship to all, without exception, events and matters of life.[15]

Similarly, Marian Zdziechowski, one of the deepest thinkers of the present day, although an inferior politician, in his work titled *Kościół* [The Church], published in Cracow last year, expresses himself thus:

About our religious shallowness I can speak from personal experience. Religious questions attracted me from childhood but I felt isolated among my age mates. For some, religion was brought from home by habit, others did not have it at all, or easily lost it and went over to the camp of its enemies.[16]

Finally I will quote the words of Prof. Kazimierz Morawski, the President of the Cracow Academy in Cracow, who in an article in *Przegląd Powszechny* [Universal Review] writes:

We stopped arguing that a culture which bypasses the great and eternal is condemned to shallowness and sterility. . . . Inquiring into divinity and divine things is always proof of the flight of energy, thought and sensibility.[17]

But what can be the cause of this religious sterility, religious dormancy, of the instinct in Polish society? Perhaps I will make a mistake when I say that the leading cause of this strange state of affairs is the dominance by the system of religious beliefs of the Roman Church. This religion grew out of pagan ideas and Jewish beliefs that God is a powerful being, but a vengeful one, that it is possible to placate Him with offerings and gifts, and especially that

---

[15]Jadwiga Marcinowska (1872-1943), *Wartości twórcze religijnej myśli polskiej* [The Creative Values of Polish Religious Thought] (Warsaw: Aurion, 1922).

[16]Marian Zdziechowski (1861-1938), *Kościół* [The Church] (Cracow), p. 21.

[17]Kazimierz Morawski (1852-1925), classical philologist, Rector of the Jagiellonian University and President of the Polish Academy of Sciences.

it is possible to ransom oneself through the mediation of priests. This religion has entered to some degree into the veins and blood of the Polish nation.

The Roman religion is a religion of dogmas, that is, of fixed religious laws determining certain views of God, the human soul, the destiny of humankind, present and future life, the Church, and the relationship of humankind to the Church.

Among these dogmas is one most important, and that is the destiny of humankind. It says that God created humankind in His image and likeness. He created it perfect but unhappy. Then He corrected His work when He gave to Adam, Eve, his life's companion, who at the prompting of satan became the cause of the tragedy of humankind. They were cast out of the garden of paradise. The terrible human history begins, drenched in tears and blood. God punishes rebellious humanity with a flood. But the established bloody sacrifices are to propitiate Him. The clergy lived from the offerings and took advantage of the poor people.

And Christ Jesus appears and declares war with all who with their lying and hypocrisy gave a false picture of God. Christ teaches that God is a Father, that people are brothers, that the happiness of humankind depends on knowing the Highest Being and entering into a close sincere relationship with Him through faith, prayer and the noble deeds flowing from this faith.

The Christian religion gives us the most perfect convictions of the unity of the human spirit with the first cause of existence, with the inexpressible cause of everything, with God. In this adheres the principle of the endless tendency towards learning the truth, the progress of the soul and life. This is a state of the dynamic development of the human soul, the perfecting of the individual person, the nation and all humankind.

Address at the Reception of Delegate Łaszczyński at the Town Hall in Scranton[18]

One of the greatest achievements of modern civilization is respect and honor for human labor. In the past, labor was undervalued, work was shameful, and what goes with that, working people were mistreated and abused. There was kowtowing and bowing before those who did not need to work hard, and those who did work hard and with their toil created wealth and fed others were regarded as half-free or slaves. Even the greatest of the ancient thinkers such as Plato and Aristotle regarded this economic system as just and the only one recommended, in which a minority rules and possesses full rights of citizenship and the majority works and produces. This majority of people had no rights, it was not free. And such a system lasted whole ages.

Truly Jesus Christ came on earth as the greatest teacher of humankind, the spiritual regenerator, and he condemned a social order based on cruelty and injustice, and His immediate disciples tried to create a new order, the Kingdom of God on earth, but the exponents of force and exploitation soon managed to gain for themselves the leaders of the Christian Church and impose on them their points of view. And the entire Middle Ages, that is, for about a thousand years more, this unjust system was tolerated, this order in which two castes, that is, the magnates, nobles and clergy, possessed rights and privileges; townspeople had limited rights, but the great masses of peasants and laborers were without rights, without influence whatsoever. It was not even permitted to change one's lord. One was tied to the field or to the workplace like some kind of thing without a soul.

Not until the beginning of the nineteenth century were the

---

[18]November 30, 1919. Maciej Łacszczyński of Dąbrowa Górnicza was the editor of a labor newspaper and a delegate to the International Conference of Workers held in Washington. Among those taking part in the event in Scranton were Congressman J. Farr and J. Dempsey, President of the United Mine Workers Union, with a reported audience of 3000 persons. Father Thaddeus Jakimowicz spoke in English.

commandments of Christ the Lord remembered, His teaching about the worthiness and value of labor. But it was not the priests, not the bishops, not the pope — these representatives of the Christian Church — who recalled this splendid teaching of Christ about the value of the human soul and labor, but lay people, first in England, then in France. It began to be taught that work is the foundation of the social structure, that work is the source of wealth, prosperity and happiness, and what goes with this, that it is not the nobility, not the magnates, not those presently ruling who should be the ruling class, but if there is to be a ruling class then it should be the working class.

And from that time, that is, more or less from the middle of the last century, begins the organization of workers on a larger scale in the name of the rights of man, in the name of the value and worthiness of labor. Everything that workers did in the name of their slogans was good.

And today one may say boldly that the cause of labor is the most important one, and that progress, the development and happiness of the whole nation, of all mankind, depends on its just resolution. Workers today have more privileges than they have ever had.

In this reasonable and just struggle for rights, bread for the family and education for children, for common control of the wealth created by the worker, our holy Church stands before the worker like a pillar of fire, and the hand of Christ blesses him in his work.

Sermon On The Church[19]

> _This day salvation has come to this house._
> Luke 19:9

There are solemn, holy, days in life that one never forgets. Such a moment for me and for you who established this Church was the moment when seventeen years ago I celebrated the first service in the basement — the crypt of this church. United then in common prayer, in the faith of the Holy Mass, strengthened by the Word of God, we pledged ourselves to stand together, to work together for the glory of God and for the sanctification of our souls.

So many years have passed since that solemn moment. We have lived through so many trials, afflictions. Storms of hatred and human perversity raged over the Church. But it stood unmoved like a monument of the faith, ardor and love of the Polish people.

Not everyone endured the seventeen years in this toil and struggle. Some, like chaff, fell away when the wind of trial and temptation blew. Others lost interest and stood to the side, like the foreign, the cold and the uninterested. And others clearly left — because they had to leave, they fell asleep in the sleep of death, placed in the cemetery. They left through the portal of their church, covered with tears, honored by the Church and their family like brave soldiers, heroes awaiting eternal reward beyond the grave.

We the living remain, faithful members and confident that in time new legions of the people of God will join us. For today we constitute a considerable grouping, many parishes.

When today we observe the past times, what kind of task do we assign ourselves, what goal for the work and endeavors of the future. The same as in the past. In the Revelation of St. John we read: _God will dwell with them, and they will be His people, and He, God, will be their God._[20] In these words lies the entire meaning

---

[19]March 22, 1914.
[20]Paraphrased. See Apocalypse of St. John 21:3.

of our past and present work. We built a house of God. We desired God to come down and live among us. And He fulfilled our desires. He lived with us through seventeen years like a Father among His children, like a Lord with His subjects, as the Savior and Healer among those needing help, encouragement and rescue. He came to us spiritually through the Word of God, that Word which created the world. Though in an unfit human form, it spread here, in this temple, awakening in our hearts this faith, this love, this veneration, this awe and yearning.

Here Christ led us, distributed graces, and through the Holy Sacraments fed us all, all the children of His Church. When the first time they came in youth in a white dress with a myrtle wreath, then in adulthood, and finally when strength failed or mortal illness has thrown us upon the bed of pain, Christ Jesus will come to us and gather us to eternal happiness.

On the Love of God in the Human Heart

Who abides in love, abides in God, and God in him.
1 John 4:16

The greatest adornment of human life is love. Love is a stimulus to life. What would life be for a child without the love of its mother? What would life be in the family, in the Church and in humanity?

And if human love is so necessary, how much more so is the love of God. Yet it is so difficult to speak of the love of God. However, I will try to say a few words about the topic of the lack of and the power of God's love in the human heart.

Among all the matters in the world, the greatest love is God, the Creator and Judge.

Let us look around the world and at all those beings whom we should love in gratitude for benefits received and we will conclude that the first benefactor is God. Let us look at all creations the possession of which would make us most happy — and what are they in comparison to the perfection of God? God ingrained this love in all creatures but the most in the human soul and heart.

But can it always be found? Does this love of God adhere in our body and heart?

The Commandment says: *You shall love the Lord thy God with your whole heart, and with your whole soul . . . and with your whole strength.*[21]

But do we act according to this injunction of Christ the Lord? Unfortunately, so rarely! And what is the cause of this?

First, weak faith. God is an invisible being and we are good at loving that which is visible, that which falls before our senses. That is why a person loves money, wealth.

Therefore if we wish to uplift ourselves, then first of all let us strengthen in ourselves faith in God, in justice and in holiness. Let us follow St. Augustine: "I ran," says this great confessor of grace, "and I sought creatures to which I could offer love." We must rise above this squalid land.

A second barrier to the love of God is a person's self-centeredness. A person races around the world to satisfy his urges, but to no avail.

What a great force of love is in the human heart. Christ said: *I have come to cast fire upon the earth, and want only that it be kindled?* This fire is love. But how frightening was that current pagan and Jewish world. Sensuality, conceit, licentiousness, bloodlust ruled. And despite this Christ said: *I have come to cast fire.* [22]

How did Christ ignite this fire?

First in a certain small group of selected people. Not only such souls as St. John but also sinners, and the openly sinful Mary Magdalene. Wealthy and proud people for the love of God cast aside palaces and riches and joined with the poor and persecuted

---

[21]Mark 12:30.
[22]Luke 13:49.

confessors of Jesus Christ.

Above the heads of the Christians a storm rages. All the pagan and Roman and Jewish powers pledged to break those in whose hearts burned the fire of holy love.

Of no effect were the tortures, the burning flames, the sword and death — the love of God and Jesus Christ were stronger.

And in the human heart what miracles this love of God causes! What a strengthened force it is, of joy and of happiness.

St. Paul says that the power of God's love in the human heart is so great that no one is able to tear away from this love.

Who shall separate me [us] from the love of Christ? Shall . . . distress, or persecution, or hunger, or nakedness, or danger, or the sword?[23]

No, neither death nor life . . . will be able to separate me [us] from the love of God.[24]

The love of God in the human heart remains forever and for the ages. Human love is not sure, not certain. Everything on earth is temporary, mediocrity upon mediocrity, but the love of God no one can tear out of the human heart, or destroy.

And do you have such love in your souls and hearts, does this holy fire spark in you, Brothers and Sisters?

If so, then you are happy and blessed a hundredfold. And if not, you are impoverished and unhappy.

The hour will come when you will have to depart this earth and all its doings, when you will abandon everything upon which you built earthly happiness, when your body will crumble into powder and ashes, and your bones will rot. O! Then you will be mindful of the limitless love of God which is the password to heavenly happiness.

---

[23]Romans 8:35.
[24]Romans 8:39.

An Address at a Cemetery at the Blessing of a Gate[25]

We know that we have passed from death to life.
I John 3:14

Perhaps more than one will be offended that at the opening of a new cemetery gate so many ceremonies and processions and prayers are conducted. The thing is that this cemetery portal is a symbol, a sign, that depicts for us that gate through which we pass into eternity.

And therefore we have acted properly when we gathered together to reflect on the meaning of this gate which leads us through the cemetery grave to future life — the gate of eternity.

Almost all people pass through a cemetery gate, but do all pass to salvation, to eternal peace? Unfortunately, no! For some die to live further, only, a better life, fuller, more perfect. And others die without hope of resurrection, not to a better life. These through death unite with God, with Jesus Christ, and those distance themselves even further from Him.

Who are these first and those others, the unfortunates? These first are they who follow after Christ in this world, and those others are they who scorn Him. Jesus Christ said of Himself: *I am the resurrection and the life . . . I am the way and the truth . . . who follows after . . . me does not err but will find life eternal.*[26] And what are the characteristics of those who follow after Christ, who later, through the cemetery gate, pass into eternal happiness?

They have, first, faith in Him as the Messiah and the Mediator, and they act in accordance with this faith. *Everyone who believes,* says St. John, *that Jesus is the Christ is born of God.*[27]

And in the region of Caesar Philipi Jesus asked who people thought the Son of Man is. And Peter answered: *You are the Son of the Living God.* And Christ replied: *Blessed are you, Simon bar*

---

[25] April 23, 1908.

[26] John 11:25; John 14:6.

[27] I John 5:1.

Jona.[28]

This faith in the mission of Jesus Christ, in His merits, causes that our life has value and merit before God for life eternal.

A second sign of our election is work for the benefit of humankind, for justice, according to which, as St. John says further: *Everyone who acts justly is born of God, and who loves his brothers is passed from death to life.*[29]

St. Wojciech [St. Adalbert][30]

For in Christ Jesus, through the Gospel, I gave you birth.
I Corinthians 4:15

What once St. Paul, the Apostle to Nations, could say about himself, that he became the spiritual father of many settlements in Asia and Europe, St. Wojciech could repeat about himself in respect to our Fatherland, Poland. He was the apostle and father of our Polish nation in Christ Jesus our Lord.

Just as once the Apostles at Christ's words abandoned their family territories and scattered over the wide world to tell about the Gospel and to carry to the pagan people the light of God's truth and to show them the road leading to salvation, so did St. Wojciech, the patron of our nation, abandon his family land, Bohemia, and the episcopal see in Prague, and come to Poland to speak there about Jesus Christ crucified. And then, when he had sufficiently sowed God's seeds in Gniezno and Cracow, he went to the north among the pagans — the Prussians — and there died a martyr's death.[31]

---

[28] Matthew 16:16-17.

[29] I John 3:14.

[30]1902.

[31]The Prussians were a pagan Baltic tribe who eventually were destroyed. The term was later given to the Germans who settled in that area. Gniezno was Poland's first capital and the site of its first archepiscopal see. The Polish state formally accepted Christianity in 966.

St. Wojciech was born in Bohemia in Libicz in the year 950, therefore 952 years ago, of his father Sławnik, a wealthy count having great landholdings on the banks of the river Cydlin and the Elbe, and of his mother Strzerysława, from the house of Urol. In the home of his parents Wojciech received his primary education together with his brothers Sobobor, Poraj, Czesław, and Radzyn.[32] When he was seven years old, he became seriously ill and his mother made an oath at that time that if Wojciech should become well, she would dedicate him to the priesthood. The child recovered and then his parents placed him in the at-the-time famous school in Dziewin, which was blossoming under the care of the saintly Bishop Adalbert.

In that school Wojciech spent nine years and progressed in his studies and moral virtue, so that he became beloved by all his companions. After the death of Bishop Adalbert, Wojciech returned to Prague and was there ordained a priest. The young priest soon so shone with fervor and a virtuous life that he attracted the attention even of the Czech King Bolesław II. It was nothing strange, then, that in the year 982, after the death of Bishop Dytenych, Wojciech was unanimously chosen a bishop even though he was only 32. And the entire Czech nation received this choice joyously, for Wojciech was only the first Czech bishop, all those previous being Germans.

With the placing of the bishop's miter on his head, Wojciech accepted on his shoulders terribly heavy duties. It is necessary for us to remember that the Czech nation at that time, even though it was already Christian, that Christianity was rather more superficial than internal and engaged in life.

Not even a hundred years had passed (871) since the Czech Prince Bożywój and his wife Ludmila had received baptism from the hands of the great apostle of the Slavic peoples, Methodius.[33]

---

[32]The Czech names were given in a Polish version by Bishop Hodur.
[33]St. Methodius (d. 885) and his brother, St. Cyril (d. 869), are considered the "Apostles to the Slavs" or to eastern Europe in general. They translated the Scriptures into the Slavic language and established a Slavic Rite.

Here and there the Czech people were still secretly placing offerings to the pagan gods and instead of the names of Jesus Christ and the Most Holy Virgin Mary called upon the names of those gods. And with this they led a life full of obscenity and carnality. The histories tell of two main faults. The Czech nation at that time indulged in carnality or licentiousness, and sinful drunkenness. It could be said of it in the words of the Holy Scripture: *Every heart is corrupted, every head is sick.*[34]

It is not surprising, then, when he observed this terrible state of those people, Bishop Wojciech decided to haul them up from the gutter. He and his priests traveled throughout the land calling the people to virtue, corrected them and punished the incorrigible. But, unfortunately, what was the result of this apostolic fervor? That the nation used to disgrace, to blasphemy, to drunkenness, and gross pagan practices, became enraged and expelled its holy and fervent father and shepherd. With pain in his heart and with tearful eyes Wojciech left his ungrateful native land and went into exile.

O poor holy man, expelled from his fatherland by his own impious and criminal people!

But if you rose from the grave and came to us in Poland, would you find a different people?

On the Need for Prayer[35]

Whoever knows how to pray well also knows how to live well.
St. Augustine

In the previous teaching I pointed out two of the most important duties a person has: to recognize God and to serve Him; and one kind of service is prayer.

What is prayer? From where do we know that it is necessary to

[34]Isaias 1:5. *The whole head is sick, and the whole heart is sad.*
[35]1902.

pray?

From the mind, the heart and the Holy Scripture.

When Christ was praying, His disciples came to Him and asked: *Lord, teach us to pray.*   Christ answered them: *In this manner therefore shall you pray: Our Father, Who art in heaven, hallowed be Thy name . . . Thy will be done on earth as it is in heaven . . . .* [36]

Is prayer necessary for salvation?   Is it a sin to omit prayer? What benefits does prayer bring?

On Preparation for Prayer

Verily, verily, I say unto you, that whatsoever you shall ask of My Father in heaven, you shall receive.
John 16:23[37]

Yesterday I spoke of the need for prayer and also the benefit of prayer, today, however, on what prayer should be to be pleasing to God, valid and effective.

I. It is necessary to prepare for prayer.

Before prayer, prepare your soul, and be not as a person that tempts God.[38] To tempt God means to speak beautifully but to do wrong.

Is kneeling during prayer necessary?   There are differing customs, but we know that Solomon, the prophets, Christ the Lord, and the Apostles knelt in prayer.

II. It is necessary to be in a state of grace.

If you abide in Me and My words abide in you . . . whatsoever you ask, you will receive. [39]

III. To plead for a proper thing.

---

[36]Matthew 6:9.
[37]*If you ask the Father anything in my name, He will give it to you.*
[38]Ecclesiaticus 18:23.
[39]See John 15:10 and 16.

In addition, prayer should be humble, with devotion, with faith, trust, and in the name of Christ.

On the Angelic Salutation

Hail Mary.
Luke 1:28

Second to the Lord's Prayer, composed by the Lord Jesus Himself, the most beautiful prayer is the Angelic Salutation: Why?

1. It has to do with the Most Holy Virgin Mary.
2. It was composed in the cause of the Holy Spirit.

It was also composed:

1. By the Archangel Gabriel.
2. By St. Elizabeth.
3. By the Church.

What purpose does this prayer have? To honor the Most Holy Virgin Mary.

What do the words *Hail Mary* mean? Greeting, joy.

A Speech Given at the Blessing of the Polish National Church in Nanticoke[40]

Where two or three are gathered in my name,
there I am in the midst of them.
Matthew 18:20[41]

These words came to mind today and I would wish them to cling also in your hearts and thoughts and when you return to your homes that they might occur to you and strengthen you in your

---

[40]August 25, 1907.

[41]An example of the variations between the Polish of Wujek and the English of the Confraternity text, which reads: "for my sake." Such variations are frequent.

faith and love in the national wandering in the diaspora. For these words are for us of more particular attention because they are the source of that value of sanctifying humankind about which bishops and priests speak so little, and which always pose a fundamental difference between the old Roman Church and the Polish National Church.

In the old Church may often be heard: Prayer, the Sacraments, the Holy Mass, are valid in this place conducted by such a bishop or priest and by that one are even more valid, but we feel that the great significance of the Holy Mass comes from Christ, from God. *Where two or three are gathered in my name, there I am in the midst of them.*

If, therefore, God abides everywhere, then why build churches? Because the church is a collective place to honor God, it is a visible monument of the love and gratitude of the nation in serving the Most High Being, and the Church is also the nation's school. God likes to visit temples raised by human hands.

When King Solomon begged the God of Israel to raise up the Jerusalem temple, the Lord said to him:

I chose for Myself this place for a house of offering, and the prayers of one who comes there will be heard, because I chose this place so that My Name may be honored forever. [42]

Yet beyond this, the Church is to be a school and a path for the nation. Just as an individual person errs, departs from the true path, so the Church as school and path leads a person to God.

The Jewish nation betrayed God and broke His Commandments and then God sent prophets who with inspired words condemned the wrong and induced the people to return to the true God.

And is not our nation a frightening example of betrayal of the Most High Being of God, who is the highest good on earth?

---

[42]See II Paralipomenon (II Chronicles) 7:12 and 16.

It must be said, however, that our nation raised up large and splendid temples to God, in which the Polish people gave honor and prayed that our Fatherland might be free, great, powerful, and independent.

Speech in Priceburg on the Occasion of the Twenty-first Anniversary of the Rising of the National Parish[43]

We are God's fellow workers.
I Corinthians 3:9

There are certain moments in the lives of individual persons and of large associations when some internal voice encourages more attentive reflection. These are pivotal moments and the remembrance of crucial times.

Today we are observing in Priceburg a remembrance of such a pivotal moment, the foundation of a National Church. And to this holy day you have invited those closest to you. And me, your closest of the close, because he who twenty-one years ago called you to the great work and was a vigilant witness of your labor, your fervor, endeavors, reversals and errors, progress and efforts in the name of a most holy matter.

When I was thinking about a suitable talk, I wanted to find appropriate expressions and titles for you, my Dear Brothers and Sisters, who have endured, believed in the greatness and importance of the cause of the National Church. And I found in the Holy Scripture a suitable term touching you all, fellow workers of God.

Therefore we read in the letter of St. Paul the Apostle to the Corinthians: *We are God's fellow workers. . . . Do you not know that you are the temple of God and that the Spirit dwells in you?*[44] This sentence which the great Apostle of nations said to his friends

---

[43] July 13, 1919. Priceburg today is named Dickson City, Pennsylvania.
[44] I Corinthians 3:9 and 17.

in Corinth I can adapt to my friends and fellow workers in the National Church across America, for my friends are to fulfill the same work which the contemporaries of the Apostle Paul fulfilled.

In truth Christ the Lord named as His co-votaries in the first rank those who left their homes for Him, but have we not also to in a certain respect done the same for Him, His holy cause and our Church?

O it is so! When we decided to leave the old Church twenty-one years ago, this was an important step. In more than one home division occurred.

The Apostles were to carry the light of the Gospel of God among the pagans and the Jews who in truth knew the name of God but who had erroneous concepts of Him.

They believed that God is above all the God of the Jews, vengeful, jealous, terrible.

Whereas the National Church opened the gate of love and mercy. The teaching of the National Church instructs that God is the source of all good. Jesus Christ is the mediator between God and humanity.

The majority of Roman priests are pharisees. They speak of Christ's love, but they do not imitate Him.

The priests of the old Church were indifferent to the Polish nation's affairs.

The National Church began to awaken love of Poland, of the Polish language. It raised it to the altar, made it a vessel of prayer, of holy rites. In prayers of supplication the National Church did unite and does unite the people with God.

Such a service the Polish National Church did fulfill and continues to fulfill.

Address at the Observance of the Constitution of the Third of May in Wilkes-Barre[45]

When I see gathered before me so many honorable Countrymen and Countrywomen I do not presume even for a moment that simply common curiosity inclined you to appear in this hall and a desire to hear some kind of jabberwocky.

O no! To this hall love of the Fatherland commanded you to come. Our forefathers spilled their blood for the freedom of the Fatherland at Racławice, Warsaw, Miechów, Ostrołęka; from the Atlantic Ocean to the Volga River.

Therefore this memory of our land, for her past and her peaceful actions, also commanded us to gather and to bow our heads before the small group of patriotic people who lived more than a hundred years ago. Though they could not save the Fatherland from its threatening loss, they highlighted its end and by establishing new humane and more just laws they earned immortality for themselves.

O yes, Countrymen and Countrywomen! The Constitution of the Third of May was a great, noble act. It was a step forward in the history of the Polish nation.

Poland before 1772 was a weak country, gangrened by the anarchy of the nobility, the indifference of spirit, a people without laws living in poverty, debasement and ignorance.

The Constitution of the Third of May gives to the city dwellers rights of citizenship, it promises the country folk care and justice. Therefore let us also, representatives of the people in diaspora, always keep in memory the names of the creators of the Constitution: Kołłątaj, Staszyc, Potocki, Małachowski.[46] It is our

---

[45]May 11, 1902, in Wlkes-Barre, Pennsylvania. The Polish Constitution of the Third of May, enacted in 1791, was the first modern national constitution in Europe and second only to that of the United States of America. The entire constitution included two other sections previously approved in March and April of that year.

[46]Hugo Kołłątaj (1750-1812), Stanisław Staszyc (or Staszic) (1755-1826), Ignacy Potocki (1750-1809), Stanisław Małachowski (1736-1809).

duty to give honor to these heroes.   Our love of our beloved Fatherland should never end.

No, Brothers and Sisters!   Although we are plain and poor, even we are called to action.

And we, what are we to do? What threatens us? Hardness of heart, arguments, hatred, wasted energy, indifference — what will Poland give me?

O do not say that! It is the land of our forefathers. It is our heart!

O Polish land, our Mother, I shall never forget you!

Address in Wilkes-Barre, Pennsylvania[47]

I came here to stir a few matters, some subjects, that seem to me to be interesting and important, and which are so rarely discussed in our society.

When a person travels across the wide world he notices practically everywhere, especially in large cities, splendid churches erected to the glory of Jesus Christ. Some are in the Greek style or basilicas, others are Gothic or Baroque.

These churches claim that they believe in God and Jesus Christ, that Christ the Lord is their master and Savior, but nevertheless they hate each other. When on the street an Orthodox pope meets with a Roman priest, they do not speak to one another. Or when by accident a Roman priest comes together with a Polish National, he pretends that he does not see him, or abuses him with a word, or spits before him, or in another way demonstrates his hatred and rancor.

Are all of these priests, all these votaries, truly worshipers of the same God, adherents and disciples of the same Master, Jesus Christ?

If Christ should find Himself once again on earth, He would

---

[47] [1902].

deny those who have hatred, who turn away from a brother only because he folds his hands differently in prayer or prays from a different book.

When Christ gathered his disciples before the bloody Passion, He said to them these memorable words: *A new commandment I give you, that you love one another . . . . By this will all men know you are My disciples, if you have love one another.*[48]

Already the prophet Malachi called: *Have we not all one Father? Has not one God created us?*[49] And St. John in the thought of Christ says, *that God is love and whosoever loves his brother,* humanity, *is a child of God, and anyone who says, "I love God," and hates his brother, he is a liar.*[50]

It is necessary to love not only those who are of the same political, social, religious conviction. We have proof in the parable of Christ about the Samaritan, a person hated by Jews, but who brings help to his neighbor attacked by robbers.

And today?

Today it is not love that characterizes the various Churches and the people of the various Churches but hated and contempt.

And where to seek the cause of this perversion of the uplifting teachings about the love of neighbor, human justice, where is the cause of these wars which have harassed the Christian nations?

I see the cause of this state in the teaching of Roman priests in their pride and the idolatry of the Roman Church.

If I touch this matter it is not to degrade the Roman Church but to indicate the errors, the defects, which degrade a person and insult Christ the Lord.

They do not place in the hands of the people the Holy Scripture. They dislodged Christ the Lord and sat the Pope. We must condemn this as an unChristian status.

Nevertheless Christ the Lord commanded His disciples to call themselves *of quiet and humble heart.* Christ the Lord said: *Verily*

---

[48]John 13:34-35.
[49]Malachias 2:10.
[50]See I John 3: and 1: 4:9, 16 and 20.

I say to you, if you do not become as children, you will not enter into the heavenly kingdom.[51]

Address in New York[52]

Invited, by the committee of the parish organizing itself, to speak at one of the meetings, I wavered in accepting the invitation only for the reason that I do not have presently a priest who could effectively take up battle with the Roman priests in New York and the vicinity. If I am here today, it is only to thank the honorable gentlemen for remembering me, and, on the other hand, to explain my views on the matter of the Church, to present the difficulties that come to be combated, and the benefits the Polish people will gain from the founding of the Polish Catholic or National Church.

Although I well know that for you gentlemen this national movement in the Church, of which I am a representative, is not alien, looking at it from a distance you may have a completely different notion of our efforts not corresponding with the actual state of affairs.

I will begin from the incentives which inclined me to cast aside the Roman Church and found the National Church in Scranton. Right at the beginning I will admit that I did this from two incentives, because of two causes. First, from personal incentives. It became too stifling in the Roman Church. When I compared the teachings of Christ, as I find them in the Holy Scripture and in the first centuries of the Church, with the teaching which today they teach from the pulpits in the Roman Church, I noticed a terrible difference.

How different seems to me the Jesus of Nazareth teaching always in Capernaum or on the shores of the Sea of Gennezaret or

---

[51]Luke 18:17. *Whoever does not accept the Kingdom of God as a little child will not enter it.*

[52]April 20, 1902. The gathering took place at Krzywacz [Krivac] Hall on 4th Street. A committee was elected to form a Polish National Catholic parish.

in the hills of Galilee. There Christ is a great friend of His nation subjugated by the Romans and taken advantage of by the Levite class. This is a friend of the poor person when He calls: *Woe unto the rich, for they will not enter the Heavenly Kingdom.*[53] This Christ is a friend of all disinherited and poor people — this is a healer of ailing humanity and a messenger of a better future, when He calls: *Blessed are they who hunger and thirst for justice.*[54]

But how differently that Roman Christ in the Catholic Church presents Himself to us, how differently His so-called Vicar lives and teaches from the Vatican. After all, he is to be the reflection of Jesus Christ, His vicar on earth. And in reality how does he present himself to us. This is a powerful lord, residing in a palace with 11,000 rooms while Jesus says that *foxes have dens . . . but the Son of Man has nowhere to lay His head.*[55] His income from Peter's Pence alone amounts to eight to ten million lira, he is carried by a guard of nobles whose each member must prove twelve generations of nobility, he distributes medals and titles, he sends ambassadors to royal and imperial courts, and he sits moping and angry because his political state was taken away from him. In a word, this old man in a triple crown sitting on a pile of gold has as much similarity to the quiet, poor Teacher of Nazareth as Morgan, a titan of Wall Street, has with a worker whose entire wealth is ten fingers and a clear conscience. As many times as I reflected on this abyss separating the Roman Church from the Church of Christ, I was very troubled. And I was disturbed even more when I looked at the history of our nation, when I saw the duplicitous role Rome played in our politics.

And here in America, how does the care of the Roman Church appear?

In one direction, and that is in the direction of Roman Catholic priests enriching themselves.

---

[53]See Luke 6:24; Matthew 19:24.
[54]Matthew 5:6.
[55]Luke 9:58.

Address in Passaic, New Jersey, at the
Observance of the January Uprising[56]

A great, blissful day will come when brother will recognize
brother. The property of all, the earth will become rich.
And the breast of the Mother-Fatherland will breath free.
Wołłowicz

It has become the custom in America to formally observe certain national anniversaries and especially the anniversaries of the Uprisings in 1830-1831 and 1863.[57]

In all larger and smaller settlements, for example in the United States, Poles gather under the leadership of priests and give honor to the heroes to point out their toil, sacrifices and spilled blood.

And we do right to honor the creators of the January Uprising because although it did not succeed, although a river of blood and tears flowed, and about 300,000 people of different social status and age were killed, this revolution nevertheless remained without greater moral meaning. It is necessary for us to remember that this January Uprising was a protest of the Polish nation, awakening to life, perhaps still not conscious, but in any case believing in Poland.

One of the leaders of the January Uprising, Zygmunt Padlewski,[58] said these memorable words on January 16, therefore only six days before the outbreak of the insurrection: "It is necessary for us to sacrifice for the salvation of the people, for the ending of the problem by the Polish nation itself."

Padlewski and his companions wanted this to be a revolution of the people, for it to include the whole nation and bring it freedom and happiness. This was then a great step in that memorable year when people fought in the name of the Fatherland to expel the oppressor.

---

[56]January 24, 1907.
[57]The November 1830 and January 1863 Uprisings occurred in the part of Poland occupied by the Russian Empire.
[58]Zygmunt Padlewski (1835-1863).

One of the resolutions was that all of its sons were equal, that the land, which to this time the peasant worked for the lords, is becoming the property of the people. These were not only political slogans but of a economic-social nature.

The January Revolution was an event of enormous importance in those times. And if it had succeeded, Poland would have been the first people's state in Europe.

For this reason, therefore, it seems to us just to honor these people. Only it is sad that this is done superficially, that the real goal of the uprising is not underscored, that is, the transformation of the nobility and clergy into people's Poland. And what is worst, that honor is given to revolutionaries of the past but the social revolution is condemned.

It is a good thing to organize religious services and commemorative evenings for those who 50, 40, 30 years ago cried: "Down with the Tsar, long live the people free," who sang:

> *And there the promised land*
> *Without tyrant and without law*
> *Under the administration of God*
> *Awaits us beyond the sea of blood.*

Revolution therefore is a historic necessity, and whoever spits on it and ridicules its makers does not know the human spirit and does not know how to go forward with the living.

Address in the National Hall in Jersey City[59]

I did not come here today to call names at the Polish-Roman priests of New Jersey and New York but to bring to the attention of this honored gathering a few of the causes which incline people to leave the Roman Catholic Church, and to indicate other roads in

---

[59] 1910. Jersey City, New Jersey.

place of those which lead from Rome and to Rome. I safeguard myself right at the start against being called an enemy of the Roman Church or of its servants, the priests. God forbid! I was myself after all a Roman priest and I was not even the worst priest, if following me several thousand people left the Roman Church at once.

For I acknowledge the meaning and mission of the Roman Church. I even acknowledge the enormous services which the Roman Church gave to human culture. But I also see the faults in this organization which disposed me to cast it aside. Every free person should belong to any organization so long as he has spiritual benefit, as long as the teaching of the Church meets the soul's desires, as long as he finds an answer to the highest questions of existence, pacification of the soul's yearnings, and national problems. If he does not find this in a given Church, he should leave it.

Every person should clearly and honestly define such matters as morality, his relationship to God and the nation. And if in his conscience he feels that he cannot put his signature to the creed of a given Church, at least to its dogmas, he should cast aside such a Church.

The greatest adornment of a person is his character. Not everyone is given talent but each of us can slowly acquire the character of a strong person if he will behave honestly with himself and will fulfill in life those principles which may be found in his mind. When it is the opposite, if between our internal life, that is, the life of the soul, and external life there is distraction, discord, then such a person is a great liar, a most unhappy person.

And of such liars, such pharisees who think one thing and do another, there is a great many in the Roman Church. And that is why life is so sad, full of spiritual conflicts. The laity especially do not believe today in their Catholic dogmas and practices.

Where today is an educated person, a wise person, who would pay attention to papal infallibility, the authority of the Church on earth, above the earth and in heaven?

And yet there remain in the Church those who do profess these truths.

The dogmas of the Roman Catholic Church have caused those nations which profess the Roman Catholic religion to decline ever more in every respect.

The best proof are Poland, Palestine, Italy, Spain, and South America.

There is no other course for the Polish people than either to reform the Roman Church, or if that cannot be, to cast off this Roman Church and find oneself one which would answer the spiritual needs of the individual's soul and the collective soul of the nation.

Address at the Time of the Celebration
in Honor of Maria Konopnicka[60]

Now, when Poland is free, it is worth considering the work of those who earned merit for this freedom. One of these chosen and luminous souls in Poland in the burdensome times of slavery was Maria Konopnicka, who was born in the year 1842 in Suwałki and died in Lwów ten years ago.

She earned merit, above all, in that she spoke to the educated and wealthy strata of the nation, to all working for the enlightenment of the people, to all the disinherited, in the conviction that we are all part of the nation that sooner or later will gain their due rights.

The greatest service Maria Konopnicka performed, however, was in awakening in the soul of the Polish woman love for her responsibilities to the nation, to the family, and yearning for all that

[60]1920. Maria Wasiłowska Konopnicka (1842-1910) was Poland's most inspirational woman poet. The Polish National Catholic Church organized a women's literary society in her honor in 1906. At the time of her death, Bishop Hodur happened to be in Poland. When the Roman Catholic Church hesitated to bury her with church services, he offered to do so, but the problem was then quickly resolved.

is noble, beautiful and good.

Maria Konopnicka tried to point out that the time has passed when a woman tended the home hearth knowing nothing about the world. But new times have come when a woman must be a fellow worker with her husband. She must know the hard responsibilities tied to this life, and share with her husband fate good and bad, to stand by his side, trust him, and uplift his spirit.

In addition, Konopnicka encourages discipline. She knows that Polish women are noble but little disciplined.

The teachings of Maria Konopnicka did not go for naught. In the time of the five-year war [World War I] Polish women distinguished themselves with courage, sacrifice and self-denial, and drew the eyes of the whole world.

Address During the Blessing of the Altars in Scranton[61]

> *If I should speak with the tongues of men and of angels,*
> *but do not have charity . . . I am nothing.*
> 1 Corinthians 13:1 and 2

Two religious ideas are pressing us all on the occasion of the anniversary of the beginning of the Polish National Church and the blessing of the altars: the ideas of sacrificing oneself and of penance.

An altar is a place of offering, the sacrifice of something to the highest Being. The term *altar* comes from the Latin word *alta,* meaning altar, a raised place, a height.

From the first moment when humankind recognized its origin in and dependence on God, it wanted His help. The various kinds of altar offerings are only the endless striving of humankind towards God, the seeking of His grace, forgiveness and peace of soul.

The highest and most perfect symbol of this relationship of

[61]February 28, 1920.

humankind to God and vice versa is the Christian altar. It is the place of offering, reconciliation and union. The altar of Calvary is the exemplar of our altar.

Cain and Abel, Noah, Abraham, Jacob, Moses, David, Solomon . . . sacrificed. Yet what were those sacrifices compared to the sacrifice of Christ?

He freely sacrificed Himself to give us an example of what we are to do: that we are to offer to God ourselves.

And today symbolic offerings are sacrificed in churches. However, they will not have meaning before God if we clergy and faithful do not follow after Jesus Christ, the greatest sacrificer. People argue about the forms of faith. Some say that it is necessary to profess as it was laid down in the year 325, 341, 1563, 1870 . . .

And therefore it is bad. Christ wanted a different faith, another religion. He never said that such must be the form, such the creed, these are to be your acts.

When a young wealthy man came to Him and asked: *Good Master, what good work shall I do to have eternal life?* Christ answered him: *Keep the Commandments.* [62]

Only in the Gospel of St. Matthew do we have enough examples to prove what religion is to rely on. In Chapters 5, 6 and 9 Christ says: *Blessed are the merciful, for they shall obtain mercy.* [63] (An example of active love).

In the same Chapter: *Let your light shine before men, in order that they may see your good works, and give glory to your Father in heaven.* [64]

In Chapter 7: *By their fruits you will know them.* [65]

At the end of life, what will decide our fate, happy or unhappy eternity? Good deeds, whether towards God or people. These good deeds are the fruit of love based on justice. Who does not have love is not in a state to do anything good. Perhaps one can

---

[62]Matthew 20:16 and 17.
[63]Matthew 5:7.
[64]Matthew 5:16.
[65]Matthew 7:16.

mechanically perform certain actions but they will not deserve the name of good, noble deeds. Only those which flow from love to God, and through Him for humanity, are worthy of eternal life.

Rightly too does Paul the Apostle call love the greatest power. Some thought that faith is the greatest power, but the Apostle Paul says that it is love.

Faith leads to God, the source of love. Love is the source of virtues. Can it be that a person loves God and on Sunday does not join with others giving worship to God, but blasphemes, harms his neighbors, and misuses his strength for bad purposes?

Address at the Funeral of Józefa Sarnowska[66]

Man shall go into the house of his eternity . . . and the dust return into its earth, from whence it was, and the spirit return to God, who gave it.
Ecclesiastes 12:5 and 7

It is an unappealable law, Bereaved Listeners, that each of us must return to the earth from which we came. This law was said by God to the first people when they broke the commandment. *In the sweat of your face shall you eat bread till you return to the earth.*[67]

From that time death scythes one generation after another. Under its cold, icy hand pass the wealthy and the poor, the learned and the simple. Children cry when it takes their parents. God established this order.

And yet when we speak of death and when we look at a dying person, bitter tears flow and grief seizes the heart.

And you children, sons and daughters, inexpressible pain claws your hearts when you look for the last time at the dear face of your mother. You saw how after the death of your father her strength slipped away, she weakened, and slowly approached her grave.

---

[66]August 6, 1907.
[67]Genesis 3:19.

And yet when you came to her, she denied you nothing, because she was a good mother to you and to all who knew her. Grief following the death of Józefa remains not only in the hearts of her children but also deeply in the hearts and souls of all those who knew her and who sincerely loved her.

Everyone loved her for her pious and good life and the firmness of her convictions.

She remembered the words of Jesus Christ: *Blessed are the merciful, for they shall obtain mercy.*[68]

The memory of Józefa will remain always in our hearts and souls.

"Eternal rest grant them, Lord, and eternal light shine upon them forever."

"May she rest in eternal peace!"

Address at the Funeral of Walenty Trudnowski[69]

*Blessed the man whom you choose
and take: He dwells in thy courts.*
Psalm 64:5

What great meaning in the life of the Church has a bell, the sound of the bell. Ringing the bell deserves special attention. This object installed in the church steeple, this bronze tulip, for a bell has the shape of a tulip, but when a person hears its voice, once joyous then again gloomy, sad, he will be convinced what a powerful factor in church life is a bell.

When on Sunday it calls to services, then perhaps a sick person or a nonbeliever may be able to resist its voice, and when it cries after the death of one's dearest then it carries to the soul and heart of those surviving grief and increases the pain of the loss of one's dearest.

---

[68]Matthew 5:7.
[69]April 17, 1914.

It informs first the pastor of the loss of another faithful servant of God. It moves the heart of a wife and the children at the loss of a husband and father.

What then did the cry of the bell not remind you of today when you led in the deceased Walenty. To you, wife, covered with grief, did it not remind you of fulfilled marital vows and oaths?

For more than forty years in good times and bad you went through life together, and now he is leaving you.

And you, children, sons and daughters?

He leaves you the memory of a Christian life. He leaves you an example of patience and giving oneself to the will of God.

Am I to remind you of the last months, the last days of your father's life?

It pleased God to test him with affliction.[70] He descended slowly to the grave in your eyes, faded, weakened, died — but did not curse the Creator. In the example of suffering Job, he recited: *The Lord gave, the Lord has taken away. . . . Blessed be the name of the Lord.*[71]

He has already gone from you and will never again be among you, therefore sincerely bid him farewell.

"Eternal rest grant him, Lord, and may eternal light shine on him for ages of ages."

Address at the Convening of the Special Synod[72]

First of all allow me to express joy because I can once again greet in Scranton so many good men called by their parishes to the honorable office of synod delegates. Truly, Dear Brothers, to fulfill duties in respect to the organization, in respect to the Polish

---

[70]See Isaias 48:10; I Peter 4:12ff; also I James 1:3.
[71]Job 1:21.
[72]1906. The First Special Synod of the Polish National Catholic Church was held in Scranton. The First General Synod was held in 1904, also in Scranton. The First Special Synod is sometimes referred to as the continuation of the First Synod.

National Church. This organization must be dear to you if in her name and for her good you hazard troubles and material losses. And there is not the least doubt of this. Other, even large, costs must be paid voluntarily by the delegates themselves, for the Church has always given its hand to those who with satisfaction and disinterest are ready to fulfill their duty, to come even several hundred miles and work for the consolidation of our organization. But this is also your important if difficult task. We are to consolidate, to strengthen, this work which we began almost ten years ago.

We gather in Scranton once again to accept the bylaws changed and corrected by you and secondly to raise our voice to the whole Polish nation in America and call upon it to join with us in one powerful phalanx of soldiers fighting for the cause of God and the nation.

We are all the children of one persecuted nation, both there in Europe on our own soil and here in America, condemned to slow extermination. There the brutal Prussian has been destroying the Polish folk for 150 years, and in the place of its churches establishes German villas, uses gun butts, to surround us with a spider's web of church laws, to suck out Polish blood and change us into a second and a third class of people. In light of this terrible fact, how does our nation behave in the United States? Up to this time, passively. Truly I tried to take certain steps and was even in Rome and at an Irish gathering, but these efforts did not find an echo and proper understanding among the broad masses of the Polish people. Rome laughs and promises, and the Irish mock and through their newspapers as well as through the lips of their prelates announce categorically that the rights of the Polish people in the Church cannot and will not be taken into account. The status of the Polish nation in the Roman Catholic Irish Church in America is like that of sacrificial lamb for which a monster lies in wait with basilisk eyes.

The monster is approaching step by step ever closer to the victim, its jaws already gaping and its white fangs and poisoned tongue are already visible, but the frightened, passive victim, hypnotized by the shiny green eyes of the reptile is not moving to save itself; indeed, looking into the gleaming eyes of the serpent it is pushing itself forward and laying its head in the jaws. Such serpent-monsters with gleaming, bewitching eyes but terrible intentions are the Irish bishops in America. And yet the Pole sees them smiling, robed in golden copes and miters; he hears sweet words about unity and the superiority of suffering, and he kowtows and kisses serpent-like feet because he does not understand the satanic politics of the Irish church in America.

We have seen through the intentions of the Irelands, Quigleys, Gibbonses, Thierneys, and Hobans, and we have declared war on them.[73] It does not frighten us that they are powerful, strong, backed by politics, wealth and Rome, for we have on our side a greater force, a greater power, we have the rights of the people, the rights of the human being and of Jesus Christ, the founder of the Universal Church. O yes, my Brothers, I believe deeply that if the Great Teacher of Nazareth would once again come on earth among the sons of the people and look at the palaces of kings, popes, bishops, clergy, and looked how these who call themselves vicars of Christ go today hand-in-hand with the rich, look through their fingers at the sins of magnates, and mistreat and abuse the poor and needy, if He, the good and quiet Savior, looked upon the terrible struggle which our nation is waging with the Prussian and the Tsar, and in this battle the Pope is standing on the side of the German Protestant Emperor oppressing the Catholic Polish nation, then He would weep at our fate, strike the Pope from his throne, and would speak to him in these words:

Depart from before my eyes! Are you the one who calls himself the Vicar of Christ on earth? It was I who stood among the poor and commanded the wealthy to share their wealth. Caesar ordered Me crucified for proclaiming

---

[73]All these were prelates of the Roman Catholic Church in the United States: Archbishop John Ireland (1838-1918), Archbishop James Quigley (d. 1915), Cardinal James Gibbons (1834-1921), Bishop Michael Tierney (d. 1908), and Bishop Michael J. Hoban (1853-1926).

the truth to the people. You, however, stand with kings and the wealthy, call yourself their friend, and the people you have forgotten completely. Do you not see what the thrones of the partitioners are doing to the Polish nation, do you not see what the bishops and priests are doing in America? Why do you not raise your voice against the tyrants, oppressors and torturers of the Polish nation? Why do you not punish the Irish monsignors and do not order them to return to the nation that which is its own? Why do you look upon the destruction of an unfortunate nation and remain silent, but do conspire with its enemies? Depart from before my eyes, do not call yourself the Vicar of God on earth, but the Advocate and Friend of kings and millionaires.

So spoke Christ and he blessed us in this work of salvation. *Where two or three are* united *[gathered] in my name, there I am,*[74] Jesus would promise.

And because we called together this Synod in His name for the establishment of His Church, to indicate to the Polish people the bright and sure road which leads to true freedom in the spirit of God, therefore we believe that Christ will be among us, He will enlighten us, lead us and endow us with the gifts of the Holy Spirit. We therefore remember His presence among us, and remember the lofty task which our brothers have designated for us. Let us fulfill it conscientiously, wholeheartedly, ourselves, so that the Church will not be frustrated, that these three days of your troubles and toils will result in benefit for our organization and for the glory of the Polish name. I believe in this and in this thought I open the Special Synod of the Polish National Church.

Address in Church Prior to the Oath[75]

What power is it that has brought here, Honored Brothers and Beloved in Christ? What idea has led us to this holy place before the altar of sacrifice? The idea of a Free Church, the idea of a

---

[74]See Matthew 18:20.
[75]1906. In conjunction with oath taken by the delegates to the First Special Synod.

Christian society in which Christ would be the only leader, His word the water which gives life, and the people are brothers and sisters. This is the goal for which we are bound, for which we are to work. Are you ready, Brothers, have you all gathered here in the thought that you are laborers in the vineyard of Christ and of the Nation together, and that we are to fulfill in these three days work similar to that which the Jewish priests and people did in the days of Esdras when they built the temple and in one hand held a trowel and built walls and in the other a sword in defense before the enemies of their nation?

We must further build this National shrine but also defend it before external and internal enemies who want to tear it to pieces and change it into rubble.

O may we be ready to fulfill our duty as once knights going to do battle in defense of the borders of Poland gathered in churches and before the altars pledged that they will sacrifice their possessions and life for the national cause, so we have gathered in God's church to call upon the help and light from the Spirit of all light and to pledge also before God that we will fulfill our duty conscientiously and honestly.

We clergy and lay delegates of the Polish National Church here gathered declare before God, the Source of all life, the Cause of existence and Progenitor of Light, that the charge given to us by the Polish nation we shall fulfill. We are ready to stand in defense of the pure teaching of Christ, always and everywhere. We shall defend the honor of the Holy Cross, defending it before hypocrisy, and we are ready to give our lives in defense of the truth. We pledge loyalty and love to the National Church, and respect and obedience for its laws. May Almighty God and the Most Holy Mother of His Son help us to fulfill all these duties.

Bishop Francis Hodur preaching.

SERMONS RELATED TO THE LITURGICAL CALENDAR

The Third Sunday of Advent [76]
Who are You?

The Gospel passes strange types of people before our eyes, the most noble and the plainest people, the poor and the sick, the saintly and sinners. What an odd type was the one about whom I was reading a little while ago. John the Baptist, the son of a priest, brought up in a large world, feels dissatisfied.

Why? Because a voice within continually said that the life of Jewish society is bad, godless, against God's wishes. For this reason he leaves the town and a relatively comfortable life and goes into the desert and there with prayer, fasting and meditation prepares himself for the mission to which his conscience calls him, the voice of God. He has a two-fold mission to fulfill. One, is to call the nation to the reform of its condition, that is before all the reform of its soul; the second is the preparation for the coming of Jesus Christ, the Messiah of humankind.

Therefore he calls to the king, the priests, the officials, to peasants and to workers: Repent! And then: *He is coming who is sent . . . the Lamb of God!* [77]

More than one individual living today may not like the person of John the Baptist. But that is a relative thing. However, everyone has to admit that John the Baptist came with Divine inspiration, that he fulfilled his mission, that he understood the content of his life. And that is the most important thing: to recognize the goal of life, the purpose, the value of life. States, and especially our capitalistic ones, raise a person to be a soldier, and the Bolsheviks murder with rifles and artillery those who have a

---

[76][1920].
[77]John 1:29.

different idea.

The life of a person is a great gift. Let us look at the coming into the world of a person. In a humble home there is such joy! A child is born. A little creature. In his crib he looks like half a hand, yet he fills the house with joy. In this laborer's cottage is understood the gift and the importance of human life.

And now I will lead you to another house. On a narrow bed lies a dying mother. At the head of the bed is her husband, old, gray-haired, the children around. All are crying, pierced with pain. They understand the importance of life.

The Scandinavians have a very high concept of life. They conceive of it as a tree with roots growing deep into the earth.

Secondly, life has great weight as service to God. We have contact with our God and we are to work together with Him for His glory and the perfection of humankind. If God breathed a soul into a person, what was the purpose? So that person should work for His purpose. Let John the Baptist be an example.

We must remember that the present day is the foundation of tomorrow. What you do today, you will reap tomorrow.

Shepherd's Mass Remarks[78]

And this shall be a sign to you: You will find a infan
wrapped in swaddling clothes and lying in a manger
Luke 2:12

From among nights the most blessed, the most happy is this holy night, when Jesus Christ came on earth. So many years have passed and yet at the mention of this great moment so many hearts beat with inexpressible joy, and not only the hearts of children and youth but also those of elderly and serious men. This night and these shining stars have some magic. A person feels better happier, when he is taken by thought and follows the Bethlehem

---

[78][1921]. Christmas Eve Midnight Mass, December 24.

star to find in a poor manger newborn Jesus and Joseph and the Most Holy Mother. The eyes of all turn to this holy family and at this poor crib.

How strange are the ways of God! The great work of the salvation of humankind began in a poor manger. Later that crib became the house in Nazareth, then the cross, then it became the Church in which Christ abides among us. That crib has become the altar upon which rests Christ the Lord, and the pulpit from which he speaks to us through the lips of the priest.

This poor crib changes but is always the abode and shelter of God-Man. And from this manger God's justice and love speak to you through the lips of the priest.

Today, on this holy night, we must deepen our love of newborn Christ and of his Mother Mary. May this Divine Infant extend His little hands and bless us all gathered here and our families.

On the Feast of the Nativity I[79]

Do not be afraid, for behold, I bring you good news of great joy.
Luke 2:10

If upon the birth of an individual one's dearest rejoice and organize birthday parties, how then on the birth of the Savior of the world?

All people rejoice at the coming, as was foretold by patriarchs and prophets, of Jesus Christ. For this Savior became the cause and source of the joy of millions of people who have believed in Him, have been taken by His religious principles, and have found happiness already here on earth, in this world. For Jesus Christ came to give people joy, gladness and salvation. *I have not come to judge the world, but to save the world,*[80] said Jesus Christ, *I*

---

[79] December 25,1919.
[80] John 12:47.

have come that people *[they] may have life, and have* life *[it] more* abundantly.[81]

And yet so many people are saddened by His coming, worry and curse. And the whole world is more like a house of maniacs, of wretched people, rather than the Kingdom of God.

What is the cause of this? Did Christ perhaps err when He proclaimed this Kingdom on earth and in human souls?

No! He was not mistaken, only people are mistaken in judging what is called happiness, relief and salvation.

What is called abundant life in this world and in eternity?

In the beginning, Christ the Lord pacified the needs of the human body. He healed the sick, fed the hungry, He was a healer of the body. But then He turns the attention of His listeners, that this is only a part of His mission, that the concerns of the soul were more important than those of the body. When he cured the paralyzed man, He said to him: *Sin no more, lest something worse befall you.*[82]

And the Jews whom He fed with bread and fishes, He punishes because they wanted to make Him a king because they were sated *Work not for that food which perishes, but for that which endures unto life everlasting.*[83]

Similarly He said to the Samaritan woman, that if she recognizes Him, the Savior, she will find the water of eternal life.

The world does not want to understand and accept this. The world understands only and mostly material needs. The world is as ill today as it was more than twenty centuries ago because it does not want to understand and to accept the principles of Christ the Lord, that the soul is more important than the body, that it is necessary to heal the human soul, and then the body will be healthy.

I will use a comparison: In a certain city lived two families. One family was relatively well-to-do but not concerned with

---

[81] John 10:10.
[82] John 5:15.
[83] John 6:27.

matters of the soul. The second, alternatively, did not neglect domestic economy but it cared more about spiritual treasures.

A second error of the Christian world to date has been that they listened to the Word of God, the teachings of Jesus Christ, but did not fulfill them, contrary to what Christ taught: *Be doers of the Word, and not hearers only.*[84]

On the Feast of the Nativity II[85]

When the fullness of time came, God sent His Son.
Galatians 4:4

Christ came on earth in the time of the greatest human spiritual need. Without the Savior, the world would be lost.

Let us look how humankind was disposed. There were three nations notable but different in size: The Jewish, the Roman and the Babylonian.

The Jews waited for the Messiah, they awaited liberation. Through the past thousand years they prophesied the coming Messiah, they prophesied a renewal between God and humankind. And in this awaiting the Jews lived. And so when John the Baptist came, they asked him immediately: *Who are you? Are you the Messiah.*[86]

It is true that Christ did appear, the Jews did not acknowledge the Messiah in Him, because it seemed to them that He will be like Moses. And they deceived themselves. John the Baptist [Evangelist] said: *He came unto His own, and His own received Him not.*[87]

Christ came when the world was subjugated in the political and cultural sense by the Roman and Greeks. The Romans reigned over Europe and Africa, and established peace. At the time when

---

[84]James 1:22.
[85][1919].
[86]Luke 3:15.
[87]John 1:12.

Christ the Lord came forward, peace had reigned for more than four hundred years, it was therefore a favorable time to propagate the soul and sanctify it, for such was the mission of Jesus Christ.

Humankind at that time had attained a high culture with the help of Greek and Roman scholars, but that culture was based on the false principle that some people are created to be masters and other slaves.

From this principle flowed false morality. The masters despised the slaves, and they hated them.

Christ the Lord is excluded by one and the other. They do not want to acknowledge Him as the Messiah, neither one nor the other.

Such was the sad past. Those times passed, new ones came.

But do we in our time acknowledge Christ the Lord as the Messiah? Do we live according to His spirit, His teaching?

If so, then we rejoice. May our heart and soul be merry in this great day when we celebrate the remembrance of His birth.

On Peace[88]
Sermon on the Feast of Christmas

These things I have spoken to you that . . . you may have peace.
In the world you will have affliction and troubles.
But take courage, I have overcome the world.
John 16:33

No one has ever set himself a more beautiful program on God's earth than He the anniversary of Whose birth we observe today. He came to give humankind peace of soul and heart — peace, the greatest treasure of humanity. And Christ came to give people this most precious treasure.

What does peace mean, we ask an unhappy person in prison or of one oppressed by troubles and worries, or of a rich person or of

[88]1921.

a beggar. Christ came to give peace to all.

How is it, then, that all people do not have peace, why do so many people die in despair? I will try to explain.

One time the Apostles gathered together not long before the Passion. Above the head of the Master a storm was gathering. But He spoke to them about peace, and holy peace shines from His whole being. He promises peace to His friends, but under certain conditions.

Let not your heart be troubled. You believe in God, believe also in Me. You are My friends, if you do the things which I command you. He who believes in Me, the works that I do he also shall do. . . . Whatever you ask in My name, that will I do. Peace I leave with you, my peace I give to you, not as the world gives. [89]

Christ promised to give His peace, and this is different from the peace of the world.

Three years have passed since the peace at Versailles, but there is no peace and it is not seen in the world, for human peace is uncertain, but when Christ, when God, gives a person peace, then that person is calm, internally quieted. But it is necessary to fulfill the conditions under which Christ gives peace.

I. It is necessary to fulfill the will of God, to fulfill this duty, this mission, to which we are foreordained. Christ as a human being did not live in indulgence. He was poor. He said of Himself: *The birds have their nests but the Son of Man does not have where to lay His head.* [90] The leaders of the nation saw Him as an enemy, a troublemaker, a provocation — and despite this He is full of peace.

II. The second condition is to be in harmony with Jesus Christ, because His holy teaching constitutes the essence of life. And this is the most difficult thing in the present conditions.

They do not want to govern themselves by the Christian religion. He said: *A new commandment I give you, that you should*

---

[89]John 14:1; 15:14; 14: 12-13, 27. Bishop Hodur added; "My words will be in you."
[90]Luke 9:58.

love one another as I love you.[91] He gave Himself for the world, to humankind, entirely without reservations, with all His being, so that people should do the same.

However, the world does not want this and therefore our earth is still so poor and sad.

O let us return to Christ and seek peace in Him.

Sermon for Septuagesima Sunday[92]

For the Kingdom of Heaven is like a householder who went out early in the morning to hire laborers for his vineyard.
Matthew 20:1

The most beautiful and most deserving human labor is to serve God. To serve a temporal lord, a king, or even the best regulated republic is a duty, but serving God arises freely, from the good will of a human being. In the Gospel which you just heard, the landowner does not force the laborers but invites them, *Go you also into the vineyard.*[93]

And today the Lord Christ, our Father and Judge, invites us over and over into the Kingdom of Heaven, that is, to the sanctification and perfection of our soul. He invites us to the most holy labor of a human being. We should fulfill it willingly for our own good and happiness. But how? Through what steps and experiences must this labor proceed in Christ's vineyard?

1. First, through prayer.

Prayer? I hear scoffing!

Yes! We should begin very honest task with prayer, with giving to God our thoughts and will, and before all else, our work whose purpose is our salvation. Our mind, our heart and the example of the Savior tell us to.

[91]John 13:34.
[92]1920. The first Pre-Lenten Sunday.
[93]Matthew 20:4 and 7.

Before beginning His work of salvation, Christ went into the desert where He prayed and fasted for forty days and forty nights.

Christ the Lord prayed often and sincerely.

From His heart came the signs and moans of prayer, and from His eyes tears, as He prayed for Himself and for others.

And our prayer likewise should be vital and sincere. Our devotions should come from the depths of our soul. Whether we say prayers or sing hymns, we should inspire ourselves and speak to God like a child speaks to its earthly father.

When Christ prayed before the Passion, bloody sweat appeared on His brow.

2. A second condition of work in the vineyard of Christ is that it must be orderly, systematic. A wise tradesman or factory owner or farmer works according to a certain system, an order, a plan.

And how do we do our most important work, the salvation of our soul for eternity? Only for appearance's sake? Therefore in the Church there is the need for stable organization based on a solid foundation.

When Christ began to build the Church, He selected twelve disciples and sent them to build together with Him the Kingdom of God on earth. The parish committee, the pastor of the parish, the parish school, the teachers, and all the other organizations are to be part of this building, the building of the Church of Christ. It is necessary for us to accomplish this work wisely, conscientiously and earnestly.

3. A third condition or requirement of this, our work of salvation, is our energy, our life force. With energy, with fervor, we are to do this work. Not lazily, not casually, but wholeheartedly. Just as He, our model and teacher, did. As the Holy Scripture says, Christ the Lord gave Himself entirely as a sacrifice for humankind. He did not withhold even the last drop of His dear blood for us, for humankind.

And we are to work for God and the Church in the example of Christ. our Lord and Savior.

: *Sermon Outlines and Occasional Speeches*

Sexagesima Sunday[94]

The seed is the Word of God
Luke 8:1

Mysterious is that process and relationship of a person to God. Nothing in the world has greater power than the Word of God. For the Word of God is the power of the Creator Himself manifesting itself in the human soul through the voice of the Church, our mother and father, our good friend — the inspiration of the Holy Spirit inclining us to the good life.

In the Holy Scripture we find much praise for the Word of God.

In the beginning was the Word. . . .[95]

Are not my words as a fire, says the Lord, and as a hammer that breaks the rock in pieces?[96]

Blessed are they who hear the Word of God.[97]

For it is not you who are speaking, but the Spirit of your Father who speaks through you.[98]

I have given them thy word. . . . Sanctify them in the truth. Thy word is truth.[99]

God wanted that the seed of this work and influence on the life of a person should be constant, that it might grow and give forth fruit a hundredfold. He instituted sowers, His vicars on earth: the clergy, parents, overseers.

And the seed of God falls upon the human field, but unfortunately not everything is accepted, and not everything grows for the benefit of humankind.

The Lord Christ Himself explains why this happens.

Behold, one falls on a trampled road, a second on barren land,

[94][1920].
[95]John 1:1.
[96]Jeremias 23:29.
[97]Luke 11:28.
[98]Matthew 10:20.
[99] John 17: 14. 17.

another among thorns and brambles, and only one on good and fertile soil.

The seed falls on a trampled road when people hear the Word of God but the devil comes and plucks it from their hearts.

What do these biblical words mean, who are these people to whom evil and access and ruins God's seeds?

These are people living for the world and its purposes. These are not the worst people. Indeed, they go to church, they hear the Word of God, but they do not live by Christ's principles.

How much of God's seeds have we wasted for this reason in our own lives?

The seed that fall on barren ground are those people who hear the Word of God but keep it but for a while because they do not have in themselves the basis for Christian religious life. When temptations come and torment, they fear struggle and suffering because they lack trust in the help of God.

That seed which falls among thorns are those people who for life's pleasures, for whom a short, dissipated, profligate life has greater value than a life in accordance with the principles of the Gospel of Jesus Christ. These thorns which stifle the sprouts and shoots are concern for daily life, about one's own considerations, the searching for pleasures, the satisfying of the senses, searching for wealth as a means and a goal. Enjoy life is the motto of the present time.

Finally, the last seed falls on a good field. These are those people who faithfully stand by the standard of their religious convictions, these are those people who do not live for appearances, for the world only, but who are inspired to the depths of their soul, who live and die by the Christian religion. The just live by faith. Perhaps they do not shine on earth but to them apply the words of Jesus Christ: *Come blessed . . . take possession of the Kingdom* of God *prepared for you from the foundation of the world . . . .*[100]

---

[100]Matthew 25:34.

The First Sunday of Lent[101]

Now is the acceptable time . . . now is the day of salvation.
II Corinthians 6:2

Is it possible for this time, which has come upon us, the time of the Great Lent, to be called pleasant, a time of salvation? It depends on how we understand pleasant life. If we understand life as physical pleasure, sensual, the gratification of the needs and desires of the body, the time of Lent will not be pleasant. But if we understand life in the spirit of Christian teaching, as the perfection of self by the overcoming of base motivations, then in this case the time of Lent and those lessons which Lent brings with itself — prayer, the reading of pious works, work dictated by charity — all these characteristics of Lent provide a person with spiritual satisfaction. And for this reason we call this time of approaching spring a time of rebirth, salvation. But above all this is a time to straighten out one's affairs with God, the Creator, the Judge, and Destiny.

In the course of the year, more than one of us in the struggle for existence, in work, in worries swept by fear, passion or inadequate guarding against the drives of the body, has committed a morally wrong act, one unworthy of the being of God. Through this he severed the bond with his Creator. This is the time for us to reflect on our relationship with God in this our sinful state.

Remember that sin is:

1. Forgetting about God and gratitude in regard to Him. We live from His goodness and love, surrounded by the miracles of His omnipotence. We look upon this beautiful earth, at the stars, and all this does not move us.

2. Worse yet, however, not only are we not moved to love and gratitude, we offend and insult God. If we met a person who offended his father, his mother, we would feel revulsion towards him.

---

[101][1920].

But are we any better?

Let us remind ourselves at least what God has accomplished through Jesus Christ. The Heavenly Father commands Him to seek a person. And He says: *If your sins be as scarlet, they shall be made as white as snow.*[102]

And if a person captured by His voice turns to Him, He is as happy as a shepherd who has found a lost lamb.

Sermon for Palm Sunday[103]

One of the scenes from the Holy Scripture which make most powerful impressions on us is the triumphal entrance of Jesus Christ into Jerusalem. This scene makes such a powerful impression on us through its contrast and simultaneously its simplicity.

Who is this who is riding into Jerusalem?

It is the King of Kings and the Lord of heaven and earth, and He is riding into His city on a burro surrounded by a small crowd of his humble people.

The Jewish nation gathered in Jerusalem on the occasion of the Passover wanted to see Christ the Lord to give Him honor.

Some had heard of His miracles, others had heard of His limitless wisdom, goodness, and mercy. Many thought that He is the Messiah foretold by prophets, therefore it is nothing strange that they wanted to meet Him personally, to look upon Him, to hear His speech.

News came that Christ is coming from Galilee to Jerusalem city, that on Sunday morning he will be at the north gate.

The streets swarmed. All moved towards the part of town where the entrance of God's emissary was expected.

And indeed He rides in. A small crowd of poor people is

---

[102]Isaias 1:18.
[103]April 5, 1914.

moving and among them is Jesus Christ on a donkey.

This is Jesus Christ, the Messiah of the world? Surprise lasted but a while, and then from the throats of these people burst forth a cry of happiness and joy.

Hosanna in the highest! Blessed is he who comes in the name of the Lord.[104]

Why, however, is Jesus Christ sad? Why does He not bless the people? Indeed, He weeps and says: O Jerusalem, *if you had known... the things that are for your peace. ...*[105]

Because Christ knew that this superficial reception and adoration is brief. These same people later will shout, instead of *Hosanna, crucify him!*[106]

So changeable is our human nature. But we adherents of the Polish National Church shall stand faithfully at the foot of the cross of our Master Jesus Christ.

On the Day of the Resurrection[107]
On the Dignity of a Human Being

This is the day which the Lord has made; let us be glad and rejoice at it.
Psalm 117:24

How glad a person is when after a storm good weather beams, how a person rejoices when after an illness good health comes. So did the Apostles gladden and rejoice when, after the terrifying moments of the death of the Lord Christ, the morning of the Resurrection dawned.

A terrible night of trial had come upon the tiny group of Christ's disciples before the dawn of the Resurrection, of new life, of victory over death, evil and sin — rebirth.

---

[104]Matthew 21:9; Mark 11:10; John 12:13.
[105]Luke 19:42.
[106]John 19:6; Luke 23:21; Mark 15:14.
[107]April 12, 1914.

The resurrected Christ the Lord is the symbol, the sign, the image of the victorious reborn human being. How great is the dignity of a human being!

First on account of his intellectual attributes, reason, will, and immortality. Superficially a human being is a clump of atoms. Humankind is dominating nature, steam, electricity, water. He is capable of progress, of perfecting himself. The ant, the bee, other animals, always act in one way, but a human being evolves.

Yet greater is the dignity of man in respect to his will. A human being can choose, he is not an unfree being directed by blind chance but a free being, the master of his fate.

Yet the greatest degree of perfection of a human being is his immortality, his dignity of God.

For Low Sunday

Peace to you!

Two processions, two marches, came to my attention this week. Both were interesting, each in its own way.

One march, one procession, occurred earlier in the city of Scranton and the second in New York on Monday. One was on the streets of our city and the other within the confines of a state prison. One came out of a church, circled the city of Scranton and returned to the church. The second came out of the cells of convicts, passed through the corridors of the gloomy edifice in which several thousands of breakers of the laws of God and man sit in punishment, and ended in the hall in which stood the electric chair, an instrument of death.

In the Scranton procession took part about twenty-thousand people carrying various signs on which were visible writing testifying to faith in God and Jesus Christ. Poor and rich, young and old, walked.

What was the purpose of this procession, this public demonstration?

It was an attestation by the greater part of the Protestant citizens of our city that they believe in God, that they are religious people, that they believe in Jesus Christ as the Savior.

We adherents of the National Church do not agree with the Protestants on many points, neither do we agree with their way of promulgating the Gospel. But despite this we must praise this demonstration, this procession because it is proof of the great religiousness of the American nation.

These crowds say that God exists, that Jesus Christ reigns. We want to conduct a better, Christian life. We denounce drunkenness, dissipation, incest, and now we publicly give witness to God, that we confess Him as the Creator, the Lord and Judge.

And that second march? How different it looks, what a different meaning it had. In front strode the guards, Jewish rabbis, then the chaplain, then the four condemned, four young persons, then representatives of the court and the prison. They stepped with a quiet, serious pace.

A profound silence dominated over these twenty persons. They neared the death cell. In the corner stood the electric chair and to this chair came one after another and ended his poor short life.

Why did they have to conduct that terrible procession of those four young people? Because they did not hold such a procession as was held yesterday in Scranton. Do you suppose that if those four knew God they would not have to die the terrifying death of criminals?

The Second Sunday After Easter
The Good Shepherd

> *They good shepherd lays down his life for his sheep.*
> John 10:11
> They *[I] will follow you wherever you go.*
> Matthew 8:19

The greatest Commandment says that we must love God with our whole heart, from the depths of the soul. This Commandment is easy to fulfill for all those who know God, who have a relationship with Him as children with a father. For is it difficult to love that which is to us known, dear and beautiful? Is love for father and mother a burden for good children? On the contrary, their heart needs this love.

Or is it hard to love one's fatherland, when it is known, its significance, its beauty? No, people even give their life in sacrifice when it is necessary to defend its safety and honor.

And what can be said of the love of God? St. Augustine regards the love of God as a natural and great commandment that calls to people: Love God, and then do as you will.

Christ Himself also says: *If you love me, keep my* word, that means, *keep my commandments.* [108]

But despite this people do not love God so sincerely, so warmly, with such complete surrender.

To this end, that people might know and love Him better, He sends on earth Jesus Christ. His entire mission is to work to awaken in all hearts love of God. He teaches, performs miracles, until finally He endures a martyr's death for the salvation of mankind.

Christ gave everything for mankind, to gain him, but above all he is a good shepherd. *I am the good shepherd,* Christ says of Himself. [109]

---

[108] John 14:15.
[109] John 10:11.

In the time of Christ, the occupation of shepherd was an important vocation.

The Good Shepherd gives His life for His sheep.

For the Second Sunday After Easter[110]
Jesus - The Good Shepherd

> *I am the good shepherd.*
> John 10:11

A most beautiful painting depicts Jesus Christ as the good shepherd. And in reality Jesus Christ was so. He was a teacher and pastor full of goodness, patience, zeal, and fervor for the glory of His Heavenly Father. May this picture of the dear heavenly shepherd hold fast in our heart and memory. In order to awaken our love for Him, I will devote today's sermon to a consideration of the exceptional goodness which Christ the Lord demonstrated in the course of His life on earth, namely, I will show you that His goodness was full of patience, mercy and zeal for the happiness of humankind and the glory of God.

Help me, Holy Spirit, so that my words should not fall in vain on the hearts of those listening, but that they might ignite a sacred fire of love for Jesus Christ. Intercede for me, O Mother of God, as we greet you with the words of the Archangel: *Hail Mary . . .* [111]

1. And we human beings are able to be good to others, but only so long as they show us gratitude and goodness, but to be good to a neighbor who is not inclined towards us and even is hostile — such goodness is hard to find; such goodness and gentleness of character we find in our Master and Savior, Jesus Christ.

When He lived in this world, what gratitude did he receive from people? Ridicule, contempt and suffering. He found

---

[110]1902.
[111]See Luke 1:28.

disbelief in His own country, jealousy, cold hearts, oppression, and, in the end, death on Calvary hill. Even by His disciples He was betrayed. The apostles were common people with coarse habits, naive, poorly understanding their Master, but He did not complain but lived with them like brothers, always ready to teach, to serve them.

These same apostles and disciples demanded Him to cast fire and burn the city of Samaria because it did not want to receive Him within its walls. And what did Christ reply to this? Does He perhaps send sulfur and fire on the stupid city? No. The Lord Jesus only has pity on them and even scolds the apostles that they should not be so harsh and bitter.

O wonderful and inexpressible goodness.

Let us look upon His goodness and gentleness towards the end of his life. The Jews slander Him with crime, slap Him, convict Him unjustly, tear off His robes and beat Him, put a cross on Him and drive Him to Calvary. There the madness of people leads to the last extremities, when they raise their fists at the Savior hanging on the cross and shout: "Hey, you rabblerouser," _You who destroy the temple and in three days build it up again, save yourself! . . . and we will believe_ in you.[112]

And Christ the Lord?

He prays and through lips bruised by physical and spiritual torture whispers: _Father, forgive them, for they know not what they are doing._ [113]

Look, my faithful, upon Christ's exceptional goodness and gentleness. And we, do we imitate the Lord Jesus in this respect?

O ask of your heart if it does not beat with hatred and spite, if it does not flame with anger on any occasion and last for days and weeks and sometimes for whole years in terrible bitter hatred?!

2. This goodness of our Divine Shepherd manifested itself in

---

[112]Matthew 27:40, 42.
[113]Luke 23:34.

pity. He demonstrated pity towards every living being. He hurried through villages and towns to do good. There He feeds the poor with bread, He heals the deaf, the blind, lepers. He takes pity on the unfortunate father and from the place of burial He raises his daughter, and again He sees a funeral procession coming out of the town of Nain and halting it says to the widow: *Do not weep*[114] and even though He is not asked, awakens from the dead her son, her joy and support in old age.

And before his bloody death does He pity Himself and weep for Himself? No! He takes pity on the unfortunate city of Jerusalem. And at the sight of the holy capital of David and Solomon bitter tears flow down His cheeks and words full of pity and pain rise from within his heart: O Jerusalem . . . *for days will come upon you . . . and will not leave one stone upon another.*[115]

What an inexpressible gift of God is the human heart of pity! It causes that we become similar to Jesus Christ, our Master and Savior. How many tears will a compassionate person dry, how much joy will he pour into poor and neglected people. Therefore let each of us who has a heart full of pity be blessed.

3. Christ the Lord had above all a heart full of zeal for our happiness and salvation. Surely it is not necessary to give proofs of this. We all know, our Lord and Savior, that You lived for us, suffered, and you took on the human form in order to love us, bless us, make us happy, and save us.

And are we grateful to You for Your goodness and unending warmth? Unfortunately, few are found who give glory to God. Few are those who try to imitate the Good Shepherd and to show Him gratitude. We must have on us the marks of Jesus Christ - if we are someday to triumph with Him.

And what are these marks of Christ's lambs?

There are two signs which Jesus Christ cites: In the first place He says: *My sheep follow me,* and in the second: *My sheep hear*

---

[114]Luke 7:13.
[115]Luke 19:43, 44.

my voice.[116]

To follow after Christ is to imitate Him. But do we do so? Do we go step by step after the Savior? Answer for yourselves.

The path of Jesus Christ is the path of poverty, suffering, self-denial. Whoever takes this path must overcome his flesh. But people do not want to take this path. Indeed, they flee from it, and speed down the broad road leading to riches and dissipation. But we should not remain on that road, we must take the path which Jesus Christ, the Good Shepherd, showed us. Amen.

For the Third Sunday After Easter[117]

> *A little while and you shall see me no longer*
> *. . . because I go to the Father.*
> John 16:16

How calmly Christ the Lord speaks of His death, as if it was His usual journey to Jerusalem or Capernaum. It does not frighten Him or fill Him with any great sorrow: *I go to the Father,* he says, I leave you, I will disappear from before your eyes, only to unite with you later in eternity.

It is a mystery why the heart of the Lord is not frightened because of death, and why we Christians also should not fear death.

Death according to the teachings of Christ the Lord is only a passage, a journey from this earthly life full of sadness and want to another life where our Heavenly Father will receive us as his beloved children.

Therefore how and why should we be afraid?

However, there are those who tremble at the very thought of death, who avoid the sight of a deceased person, and even are disturbed by the tolling of the bell announcing someone's death.

Who are these people? In the first place, they are all those

---

[116]John 10:27.
[117]1902.

whose heart is stuck to the world. Such people so fear even the shadow of death that the Holy Scripture says of them: *O death, how bitter is the memory of you for the person putting hope in the goods of this world.*[118]

Why? Because such people live only for the wealth which they own, or desire to own. From morning to night they think only of wealth, about multiplying it and using it. For this kind of people there is nothing holy. They do not care about the good of their soul. They laugh and ridicule. The goal of their life is money and the enjoyment and sensual pleasures bought by this money. Therefore to mention to such a person death is the same as telling him that it is the end of his happiness, that he must cast aside everything to which he is attached with heart and soul, and go into a cold, terrifying grave. Therefore such a person trembles like the King Balthazar.

How differently a person who believes strongly in Jesus Christ behaves. He does not attach great value to earthly riches. He does use the goods of this world, works and endeavors so that he and his family should never know poverty, but he does not bind heart and soul to wealth, he regards wealth as something extra in life but not as his primary goal. His first task is to not fear death, and the will of God is a virtue, perfecting oneself in God. Therefore even if he should lose his fortune, he does not complain. Moreover, such a person even feels unhappy among riches. *Woe is me,* cries the prophet David, *that my stay here is prolonged.*[119] Or St. Paul cries: *O how I am desiring to depart and to be with Christ.*[120]

We know that our life here on earth is sometimes sad. But we believe that if we live with Christ the Lord, in Christ we shall also die and with Christ we will reign in heaven.

---

[118]Ezekiel ?.
[119]Psalms 119:5.
[120]Philippians 1:23.

For the Feast of the Holy Trinity[121]

Go therefore and teach [make disciples of] all nations, baptizing them
in the name of the Father, and of the Son, and of the Holy Spirit.
Matthew 28:18[122]

One of the apparently most difficult truths of the Christian religion is that God is one in three persons. On this subject thousands of volumes have been written, disputes, wars and mutual persecutions have been conducted; that is, by those who believed in one God in one person and those who believed in God in three persons.

Today when we reflect more deeply on this teaching, it seems to us rather clear and understandable if we understand correctly the being of God.

If we accept God as the source of life, a living being, conscious of His life, and conducting everything to a perfect end, then we will easily understand the truth of the Holy Trinity.

God the Father is God when He plans the creations of the world and directs this world in its proper order. But in this world in addition to the physical order there is also a spiritual, moral one, especially as regards the human soul. The motor of this moral order in respect to humankind is God - the Savior, the second person. We remind ourselves that Jesus Christ revealed Himself to be goodness, love and mercy.

And the Lord Christ left a great task for humanity, to live in imitation of God, to perfect and save oneself.

In this work the Divine Spirit helps a person, enlightens him, touches his heart, like a field for the reception of the Gospel, awakens the sinner to sorrow, brings pangs of conscience, forgives, admonishes, leads, and directs.

Blessed is this truth of the Holy Trinity.

---

[121]June 15, 1919.
[122]An example of a variance between Wujek and the Confraternity text.

The Third Sunday After Pentecost

It is not the healthy who need a physician, but they who are sick.
Luke 5:31

Different kinds of people came to Christ the Lord but not everyone needed Him either as a Teacher, Guardian or Friend. I am not speaking about the Pharisees and Sadducees who approached Christ the Lord with unfriendly thoughts to circumvent, ridicule and debase Him.

Those persons sought enlightenment from Christ the Lord who did not find it in the teachings of the Jewish scholars and in the wisdom of the pagan philosophers. *Tell us, Master, what must we do to be saved, to be perfect.* And Christ gives them plain advice: *Do the will of God. Follow me.* [123]

Those ill in body and soul came to Him as to a doctor, and He healed and cured them.

And they departed cured of leprosy and malaria, the blind, the crippled, above all, the great sinners. They came to Him because they knew that he would reject none of them. *Come all of you to me,* said Christ the Lord.[124]

They understood that He speaks the truth, came and were not disappointed. Christ won them with His limitless goodness and love. Others felt disgust towards sinful people, but Christ the Lord, mercy and charity.

When the Jewish priests espied a flagrantly sinful woman, they wanted to stone her, but Jesus takes pity on her, admonishes and teaches her with a gentle word: *Sin no more.* [125]

And today, let us try more often love, charity, goodness, than malice — and then we will be disciples of Christ the Lord.

When the Pharisees accused Him, how did He justify Himself before them? With two parables about a lost lamb and a drachma.

---

[123]Matthew 20:21.
[124]Matthew 11:28.
[125]John 8:11.

And I have in the parish a few lambs which I should return to Christ the Lord. And I wish to say to them: "Come and return to God."

A second parable tells us that a woman found a drachma, that is, a small coin, therefore rejoiced greatly. By this the Lord Jesus wanted to tell us that if that woman was happy over a found drachma then how much more He, the Good Shepherd, will rejoice over the salvation of a human soul.

Finally, Christ the Lord justified work upon the soul of a sinful person with regard to God. And there will be more rejoicing in heaven over one sinner doing penance than over ninety-nine not needing penance. A sinful person is a lost treasure of God, an extinguished light, because God does not want the death of a sinner but that he should convert and live. God always seeks and waits patiently.

Sermon for the Sixth Sunday[126]

> *The hour is coming for everyone who kills you*
> *to think that he is offering worship to God.*
> John 16:2

Each person brings a judge with him into the world, and the judge is the conscience. This guard somewhere deep in the soul rises against everything that is bad and vile. Sometimes people can extinguish these eternal principles with their mind so that it gives wrong judgments. We see this, for example, in those Jews about whom the Lord Jesus says that if they murder they will regard this bloody act as a service to God.

And today are there no people of false conscience? O there are many and among the Polish nation.

When we raised the idea of the National Church, did not Polish priests encourage unholy acts? Were we not cursed,

---

[126]1902.

dragged before the court, attacked on the street, splattered with mud and calumny?

And all this was done and is being done by our brothers because priests are teaching that when they speak disparagingly they serve the Lord God.

O poor and blinded people, to this day they do not understand Christ's teachings!

But their conscience will activate, because it cannot be deafened forever. It awakes from time to time, and for certain in the hour of death.

It awakens and, as St. Augustine says, calls, to the sinful person: "Behold, I am. Cease insulting the Creator. Correct yourself! Otherwise woe unto you, woe!"

But people often do not listen to these exhortations, they do not want to know about them. They feel good in their sins. Just as unclean animals lie in mud and warm themselves in the sun and purr contentedly, so do people wallow in sin and crime and laugh at poor Christian believers. For to them what is God, for what morality, when they have it good, they have dollars and health, and their mouths are full.

Such people are similar to the Jews about whom the prophet Jeremiah says that they ridiculed his teachings, curses and threats, and cried: We are not afraid of your God. [127]

Are we stupid — when we act against conscience because it awakens sooner or later, and then O horror, what terrible pangs of conscience await to torture us. There are no greater pains than those caused by pangs of conscience, especially on the deathbed.

---

[127] Jeremias 5:24: *They have not said in their heart: Let us fear the Lord our God.*

For the Sixth Sunday After Pentecost[128]
The Multiplication of Bread

*I have compassion on the crowd . . .they have now
been with me three days, and have nothing to eat.*
Mark 8:2

Above the Sea of Galilee on a shore covered with a carpet of grass and flowers sat a multitude of people. They came from the farthest points of Galilee and Samaria to hear the teachings of the new prophet, Jesus Christ, about Whom they heard wonders. And they were not mistaken. From the godly lips of the Lord Christ flowed lessons sweeter that honey, and stronger than all the powers of sorcery, teachings of love, forgiveness, teachings announcing to the poor people the coming on earth of the Kingdom of God.

Behold the new time, cried Jesus Christ, of which the prophets of the old Covenant, Moses and Abraham ordered, *the becoming of the Kingdom of God on earth. Go and become co-citizens of this Kingdom. Go everyone!*

One condition was that the people should cast aside sins, that they should transform themselves through penance, that they should be reborn through faith, and a new order will come on earth — a Kingdom of love, happiness and justice.

A second condition of the coming of the Kingdom of God was that all people should desire this Kingdom and aspire to its dominion. *Concern yourselves first with the Kingdom of God and His justice, and all else will be given to you. . . . Strive to understand, that you have before you an important task, more than concern for bread and clothing, for you are children of God, straying for while on earth; you are to return to God, the final goal of happiness and eternal joy.*

Such more or less was the gist of the teachings of Christ the Lord expressed on the shore of the Sea of Galilee. And the rest of the people listened to this teaching with bated breath.

---

[128][1919].

For the Ninth Sunday After Pentecost[129]

And when He drew near and saw the city, He wept over it.
Luke 19:41

A strange thing is this phenomenon of human life . . . these tears. From somewhere in the depths of human essence flows a stream of bitter tears and it stirs the human breast in both joyous and painful moments. Let us see how these human tears flow.

Christ approaches close to Jerusalem and weeps.

In 1919, near the end of of this year, how many Polish men and women will weep upon returning to the Fatherland? These are tears of joy and celebration.

But there are also tears ripping at the heart and human soul as if with iron tongs. These are tears of pain and despair.

A few scenes on the theme of these tears clawing the human heart.

In a little village house outside of the city a mother waits for the return of her son.

On a hill stands a Polish church. The priest returns to the rectory and falls on his knees and weeps bitter tears: where are the people, the youth and children? Who led them into the wilderness, stole them from the church and from God?

Even more penetrating with sadness and pain is the scene painted by St. Luke of Christ weeping over the city of Jerusalem.

The sun was already towards the west. Christ saw before Him the beautiful city, the cheerful crowds, but he also saw the coming ruin of this city, the bad life of these people, far distant from God and His laws. Christ saw the coming punishment.

St. Luke in his Gospel says: *If you had known . . . the things that are for your peace! But now are hidden from your eyes. For the days will come upon you when your enemies will . . . surround your walls and besiege you, and will press you from every side,*

---

[129][1919].

and will throw you upon the ground and your children who are within you, and they will not leave one stone upon another, because you did not know the time of your visitation. [130]

Our National Church is not like the Roman Church — full of pride and lies. But are there not among us sometimes these same faults, pride and lies, abuses of God and the Church, neglect of religion, the soul and eternity?

If Christ should come to us today, if He emerged from the tabernacle, what would He say about us?

O Christ, come out and see how Your faithful live. If you conduct yourselves well, keep the Commandments of God, then you may be of peaceful soul, and if not — then tremble, sinners, for the punishment of God is near!

Christ wept tears of regret and love, tears of pain and self-sacrifice beyond measure. He wept in the festive moment when He was going to be led into the holy city in triumph.

There are tears which, when they well from the eyes, seem to be mixed with blood.

Eleventh Sunday After Pentecost

> *They brought to Him one deaf and dumb and entreated Him to lay His hand on him.*
> Mark 7:32

The healing of this unfortunate person by Christ the Lord is a picture of that spiritual healing which Jesus Christ effects in us through His grace and through our cooperation with grace of God. A sinful person, a person who lives in disagreement with the law of God is like a deaf-mute. Just as one may have ears that are closed to the word of God and to everything beautiful and uplifting that may be admired, so a sinful person, though his physical ears are healthy, flees from the teaching of Jesus Christ, avoids the Church

---

[130] Luke 19:42-44.

of God, does not even see those who speak to us of virtue, of God, of justice, of life in eternity.

Such a person sick in spirit should cure himself, and the first condition of future health is admitting his unfortunate state and a desire to rise from degradation. We are to do as the prodigal son, who admitted his poverty, returned to his father and obtained forgiveness, because he accused himself and confessed his fault.

We fear such accusation and such confession of sins, therefore our confession, our penance, is imperfect and does not bring us union with God.

There are three classes of people who wrongly receive the sacrament of penance:

To the first belong those who instead of blaming themselves, excuse themselves and blame their neighbors. For example, a woman unhappy in her marital life comes to confession and faults her husband.

A second class of people are those who regret sins due to current circumstances and are deaf to the voice of conscience.

The third class of people are those who do not think sincerely about correction, about changing life.

If we belong on the list of these sick people, then let us cure ourselves with the help of God and Jesus Christ.

Sermon for the Thirteenth Sunday After Pentecost[131]

> *And He said to him, "Arise and go your way,*
> *for your faith has saved you."*
> Luke 17:19

People often do not understand the meaning of faith and therefore scoff at and deride it. But in reality faith is an extraordinary power in the present life of mankind. It is the cause and source of the spiritual and moral life of humankind. Faith is

---

[131]July 19, 1919.

above all the deep conviction that God exists and that He shares Himself with a person, takes care of him and leads him to happy eternal life.

This limitless trust in God as the cause of everything and as such is an extraordinary force in human life. Faith still today causes extraordinary things.

I read that the inhabitants returned to a small French town destroyed by the Germans. Everything was razed. On a single pillar of the demolished church hung a tablet on which was written in French and Latin: Faith - *fides*. And people looked at it amazed, and with new enthusiasm took themselves to work.

Twenty-two years are passing since we took ourselves to work with trust that adequate results are certain, for a radiant and strong faith lit the way. When, tired of human perversity, I weakened, I turned for help to Him Who said: *I am the Way, the Truth and the Life.*[132] *Truly, I say unto you, he who believes in me, the works that I do he also shall do.*[133]

And a wonderful power entered me. And I continued to prophesy the Gospel of Christ. I spoke of the matter on which Christ the Lord founded the Kingdom of God on earth. I spoke of love, which is the bond of perfection of Christ's Order. I spoke of charity, which is the treasury of happiness.

And you have endured in this work because you have believed that God has ordained it and you have put into it honesty and sacrifice.

All who believed more in people than in God have fallen like chaff during threshing, but we have endured and we shall endure to our dying day.

Christ desired that people should have strong faith and promised only to such people ultimate victory.

The power of faith is presented in a picture of two houses, one built upon rock and the other on sand. The house built on rock is a

---

[132]John 14:6.
[133]John 14:12.

man of faith. Nothing will overpower it. Christ the Lord was Himself a man of extraordinary faith. Who had more opposition than Jesus Christ? He taught love of God and people. And His own family denied Him. The Jewish church declared Him a heretic and his own nation gave Him over into the hands of henchmen.

But He believed in the triumph of His holy cause, for which humankind will confess Him as its greatest friend.

Let us imagine someone among us denied by his family, or by society, that he was regarded as a social outcast. That would be very sad and painful.

How many have betrayed our holy Church for benefits merely of the moment, for a job, for human considerations.

Christ emerged triumphant through faith in His Heavenly Father. And we too through that faith shall triumph.

For the Nineteenth Sunday After Pentecost [134]

> *Then the king said to the attendants: Bind his hands and feet and cast him forth into the darkness outside, where there will be the weeping and the gnashing of teeth.*
> Matthew 22:13

The biblical king, the landlord to whom Christ the Lord compares the Heavenly Kingdom, was a good superior. He wanted good and happiness for his subjects. He therefore invited them to a wedding, to a feast, all of them without exception. He ordered cattle and poultry of all kinds prepared. But the guests did not come. The angered king ordered other people to be invited and led into the hall prepared for the feast. There were among the others some who were not dressed in party clothes. The lord looked sternly at the poorly dressed person and said: *Cast him . . . . into the darkness outside, where there will be the weeping and the*

---

[134][1920].

gnashing of teeth.

When I read again this passage in the Holy Gospel, this picture of the relationship of God to the world expressed in a simple image by Jesus Christ, it reminded me of Europe, especially those countries through which I traveled going to Poland.

It seems to me that the just judge of the world called with a great voice: *Cast mankind into the darkness outside, where there will be the weeping and the gnashing of teeth.*

The Gospel lord wanted to make his subject people happy, but when they did not want to take advantage of this, he punished them severely.

When we think about everything that happened in the world in recent years in Europe: in England, France, Germany, Czecho-slovakia, Russia, in Poland and other adjacent countries, when we focus our eyes and ears and look at the terrible pictures dripping with human blood, on those murders, tortures, on those struggles of person with person, on those shouts and laments and begging for a piece of bread, pity and mercy — nowhere did I see such mercy, such pity . . . truly the severe punishment of the Divine Lord is coming to pass: *Cast them into the darkness outside. . . .*

Christ the Lord said that where there is a body, there crows gather to tear at that body, that means, that where there are results, there must also be a cause, for the entire world is governed by laws of cause and effect. And if we look upon those terrible effects of the war in Europe, then we must seek causes.

Who did this, who brought about such great misfortunes? What kinds of errors caused this most terrible catastrophe, ignited the fire of this earthly hell. Surely I shall not be mistaken if I say that hatred, the disappearance of mercy and love, brought all this about.

The greatest human law revealed to mankind by the most important lawgiver — God Himself and His prophets, is the commandment to love God and one's neighbor. a second law united with the first one is the law of social justice. And on these two laws the entire human system is to be based. Such was and is the will of the Creator and Him Who God sent on earth as the lawgiver of the new world of Jesus Christ.

When Christ was asked which is the greatest commandment, He answered: *You shall love the Lord your God with your whole heart, with your whole soul, with your whole mind . . . and you neighbor as yourself.*[135]

And second to this law is the law of social love or justice: *A new commandment I give you, that you love one another, that as I have loved you, you also love one another.*[136]

These holy laws of the love of God and man and justice, these unavoidable moral laws of humanity were trampled in Europe, disregarded and ridiculed by the highest as by and lowest, by the simple and the learned, by popes, kings, lords, priests, peasants, and laborers.

Emperors and kings, popes, bishops, and governments based on bayonets and prison acknowledged worship of God but exploited the churches and their subjects. But these poorest people did not have even a spark of true love and justice for themselves. Therefore this terrible catastrophe came on the world, and this war. And the results of the war are: poverty, disease, destruction misery, depression, and despair.

Just as a physically sick person must seek medicine or else die so in Europe they must seek cures. And the best medicine is a better and deeper understanding of the teaching of Christ and the fulfilling of His holy will.

At the feet of Christ humanity will find health.

O may this happen as soon as possible.

Come, O Savior, Healer of the sick and miserable.

---

[135]Matthew 22:37, 39.
[136]John 13:34.

Twentieth Sunday After Pentecost [137]

> *When he heard that Jesus had come from Judea into*
> *Galilee, he went to Him and begged Him to come down*
> *and heal his son, for he was at the point of death.*
> John 4:47

Last Sunday I pointed to the failings of the individual person and all humankind in the present time. It seems to me that the state which Christ foretold is fulfilling itself, that darkness is surrounding the individual, that he does not see the saving light for himself. He claws, he struggles, he bathes in tears and blood, but he does not see any escape. *There will be the weeping and the gnashing of teeth.* [138]

In today's Gospel we see a different symbol, a different picture of a poor sinful person. On the road to Cana in Galilee, towards Capernaum, is seen a person running. He races unconsciously and terrified.

Who is this?

It is a royal courtier, but before all else the father of an ailing son. He did all that he could to save his beloved son, his child. All to no avail. In this tragic moment for him he reminded himself of Jesus Christ. His friends told him that Christ may be found not far away. Therefore he hurries, perhaps He will cheer him and save him.

Similar to this young, sick person are all people who are sick in soul and in body. They try various recommended remedies for wounds and sores of physical as well as of moral and spiritual nature. But these means are not enough or they disappoint.

People confer, they gather together in time of war and after war, to heal humanity's wounds. But this is a difficult task, for they often depart from the road that leads to the true healer — God, Him Whom He sent, Jesus Christ.

---

[137][1920].
[138]Matthew 22:13.

Everyone agrees that the causes which brought about the catastrophe were the forgetting and trampling of God's laws, moral laws. Therefore is it not necessary in order to heal humankind to return to honoring the rights of all people without exception? The unhappy bureaucrat gained that which he begged of Christ — the healing of his son. Why should today's humankind not be able to imitate him?

More than one says: Religious people were the cause of the war. Indeed, before all else Kaiser Wilhelm II was a religious man.[139] Here lies the misunderstanding in religious matters. Often the concept religion is not understood. To this time religion has been abused. It has been regarded as an external cult. A typical example is Solomon and Wilhelm II. Solomon wanted to gain God by splendor and pomp. All to no avail.

Wilhelm II left in his will a suggestion that a monarch cannot direct religion but he can use it for his political ends. Thus was it done with religion and with God.

To cure the illness which is gnawing at a person and all humankind, it is necessary to turn to God, to acknowledge His law and to live as is proper for a true Christian.

Twenty-first Sunday After Pentecost [140]

And moved with compassion, the master of that servant
released him, and forgave him the debt
Matthew 18:27

If we think about the being of God and its attributes, we come to the opinion that the most essential attributes of God are mercy and justice. These are the most beautiful attributes of God. Mercy and justice seem to be mutually exclusive but actually mutually complete one another. This deep conviction is based on the

---

[139]The Emperor of Germany, he was deposed at the end of World War I.
[140][1920].

Revelation of God and life experience, for our Heavenly Father is at once merciful and just. He punishes us and will rebuke the world for deliberately committed errors, but when we but turn to Him, with humility, with a son's plea, we will gain release from spiritual poverty.

He forgives, He gives His hand, He gives light and strength for further life and struggle and ultimate victory.

And this our faith in mercy and justice is an inexhaustible source of joy for a person.

When Moses walked through desert sands towards the new fatherland, and against him turned wild nature, enemy foreign tribes, and even lazy and godless Israeli people, then the great leader and lawgiver saw help only in God, in His mercy and justice.

God will not fail you, says Moses to the people, *for He is merciful, neither will He . . . destroy you, nor forget* you.[141]

This same conviction about mercy and justice gave strength of spirit to the prophets and teachers when they had to fight against the sins and crimes of their own nation.

Jesus Christ often underscores this character trait of God in His teachings and seals this faith in the justice and mercy of God with His dearest blood.

He tells us about this in the parable of the prodigal son and in the passage which I read to you today. God truly wants to instill in us the conviction that He is full of love and mercy, and that we should imbue ourselves with this teaching and accept it, because when we do not do this, when we will be without pity, without mercy for others, when we will be robbing our neighbors, will drink human blood and tears, then out Heavenly Father will be severe with us, a judge without mercy and we will feel the consequences of his just anger.

He has eyes and heart open to love and mercy but when we do not wish to take advantage of the time and opportunity, God will

---

[141]Deuteronomy 4:31, rearranged.

distance Himself from us, and the time of God's visitation will pass.

The great prophet Isaiah calls to the Jewish people: *Seek the Lord while He may be found, call upon Him while He is near.*[142]

This call before all is to young people. Is God not your father, has He not called you to work, service, do not your mind, heart and conscience speak of this?

O how many are those who do not want to hear the voice of God until the insect of conscience gnaws at and unsettles them.

One of the greatest poets of the world, Byron says of himself: "My life is like dried yellowed leaves. The flowers and fruit of love have passed, and for me remain only the insect of and pangs of conscience and the cancer of destruction. The fire, which burned in me, was like a volcanic island, a burning torch. Today it is like a burial mound."

By many means God calls, by goodness, by severity, again quietly to the soul in the dark of night. He calls in sermons by the casket of a friend, and through sickness and misfortune.

O may you all hear the voice of God calling to your soul and heart.

Twenty-second Sunday After Pentecost [143]

Render . . . to Caesar the things that are Caesar's,
and to God the things that are God's.
Matthew 22:21

Preachers and non-preachers explain in many ways this passage in the Holy Scripture. There are even those who on the basis of this citation want to see in Christ the Lord a supporter and friend of kings and emperors, and the enemy of the republic. Whoever, however, reflects more deeply on the picture presented

---

[142]Isaias 55:6.
[143][1920].

by the Apostle-author will admit that Christ the Lord was not concerned with supporting empires and kingdoms but rather the meaning of the duties which a person has in respect to his society.

Christ the Lord in His reply says to the representatives of the Pharisaic sect: "Give it back . . . . You ask me if one should pay the tax? Are you members of society? Do you know what obligations you have to the government?"

Is it not a reasonable thing for each one to contribute to his society, his obligations to the state without regard to what form the state may have? Christ did not teach faithfulness to emperors and kings but the fulfillment of the duties of citizenship, because on this depends the prosperity and happiness of individual persons and of society.

That what Christ said about the relationship to the state may be repeated about the relationship to every group, whether to the Church or to society.

Without intelligent and loyal work, progress and satisfaction cannot be expected. Even the Bolsheviks understand this. When the tsarist system ruled, they criticized and called for freedom and peace for the person and the working class.

But if a person has duties and obligations to individual persons and to all, or to the state, then one has even greater ones to God, the source of his life and the goal of his earthly pilgrimage.

Christian teaching says that man is created in the image and likeness of God. If we have emerged from the hand of God, if we are His creation, a part of His power and wisdom, then would it be possible to break the ties to Him as if we had nothing in common? Surely not! If we are in union with God, then from this come certain human obligations to God.

The most important duty is the fulfillment of God's will. Our reason says this, God says this most clearly in all religions. Christ proclaims this. In the "Our Father" we pray: "Thy will be done . . ."

Do not think that I have come to destroy the law . . . I have come not to destroy but to fulfill, says Christ in the Gospel. _Till heaven and earth pass away, not one jot . . . shall be lost from the_ *law.*[144]

Not everyone who says to Me, "Lord, Lord," . . .shall enter the Kingdom of Heaven, but he who does the will of my father in heaven shall enter the Kingdom of Heaven. [145]

For the Twenty-third Sunday After Pentecost[146]

As He was speaking, a ruler came to Him
*. . . saying "My daughter has now died, but come
and lay your hand on her, and she will live."*
Matthew 9:18

Perhaps there has never been such unrest as now Dissatisfaction has taken over the whole world.   The rich are fearful that they will lose their millions, the mass of the workers want a greater part of the wealth lost in the war, dissatisfied with the disaster. The victors must be watchful, because the losers will be thinking of revenge.

People contracted a peace a year ago in Versailles but there really is no true peace because in that document, which was to be the source of peaceful work, was ember of new unrest.

Is it not arresting that in the entire document, signed by 2. nations, which was to pacify the world, there was no mention of God, of Christ?

Socialists and radicals did not want to admit the name of God because they do not believe in God. Jews again did not want to admit, for they do not believe in, Jesus Christ. And so this splendid document is without the name of God and Jesus Christ.   And a sick as the world was, it remains sick. Attempts are being made gatherings are being held, they confer, but real peace is not to be seen. Is the fault not in that people consult Jesus Christ so little?

---

[144]Matthew 5:17-18.
[145]Matthew 7:21.
[146][1920].

At the time of the political gathering on Friday evening in the Forum, one of the speakers expressed a very accurate statement. "It would help in our times if in politics there was more religious guidance. Not to mix in religion but to be guided by religious principles. This would heal ailing humankind."

But let us return to the Gospel event.

In the wealthy home of the overseer of the synagogue lies a dying child, a dearest child, the happiness and joy of the life of a good person. Beside the bed stands the father, but he cannot help his child. He goes therefore to Christ. And the Divine Master hurries to the bed of the sick child because He came for the purpose to treat suffering, to uplift and to save. He came to serve ailing humankind.

If people wanted to imitate the Master and Teacher from Nazareth, how different it would be in the world. If in the human heart there was more love of one's neighbors, if we conducted ourselves with mercy and justice, would things that come to this bloody catastrophe? If things were conducted with the principle of love and justice in politics, in the factory, in the mine, in the family by husband and wife, by children towards their parents, would there be so many tears, poverty and curses? Surely not!

Unfortunately, humankind forgets the principles of the Master of peace, of goodness, or forgiveness, and believes in the power of the fist, in money. And therefore it reaps a terrible harvest. Who sows the wind, reaps the tempest.

If someone plants a bad tree, can he gather good fruit, asks Christ the Lord.

If they abuse the worker, and he then the employer, can there be social peace?

If the father in the family conducted a scandalous life and offends his children, can there be peace in such a family, joy and happiness? Or if a girl leads a thoughtless life, will she be a good wife and mother in the future?

We must go to Christ and plead for help and He will not deny assistance.

The Twenty-third Sunday After Pentecost[147]
Signs of the Times

Girl, arise.
Luke 8:54
For you shall hear of wars and rumors of wars.
Matthew 24:6

I wish to speak to you today about the signs of the times, the characteristics of the time in which we live. Because every time each epoch, has its particular traits by which it is possible to distinguish it from other epochs and times.

It is the same with a person. All people are of the same origin they have the same basic elements, soul and body, yet how people differ from one another. So do times, epochs, differ. They differ by human events, by the morality, spirit and life of a person.

To indicate these changes of the current time and to draw a lesson for us, I will bring before the eyes of those present pictures of human life from the period in which we live. Do not be afraid if these pictures are not very pleasant or encouraging.

1. Ten days ago the New York Police arrested 517 people sleeping in public parks on benches and among dry leaves, covered with rags. More than fifty among those arrested had served in the World War and wore medals on their chests. Much could be said about these people. Perhaps among them were many habitual drunkards, but there were also people who could not find work or rent a place to live. For who of us would freely seek shelter for the night on a bench in a park and cover ourselves with a rotten rag and leaves?

To these people and those like them can be applied the words of Christ the Lord, Who said of Himself: *Foxes have dens and the birds of the air have nests, but Son of Man has nowhere to lay his head.* [148]

---

[147]October 23, 1921.
[148]Luke 9:58.

Not far from Central Park stand apartment houses and places for visitors.

This is a sign of the time, a bad sign of the time. This is a great injustice, which should be removed. But who will remove it? Meetings? No! Revolutions? No!

Only the ruthless application of Christ's religion.

2. Another sign of the time is the seeking of dissipation, right to the bottom, right to the loss of mind. More than five million are without work, yet up to this time there have never been so many festive balls. People, especially the youth, dance in the evenings in order to satisfy their desires. They are drinking from the cup of dissipation because they do not believe in other moral values.

3. A third indicator of the times is the worship of money, homage to the god Mammon.

People have forgotten Christ's program for building the Kingdom of God and the creation of a moral social spirit based on the love of God and neighbor. Today each pulls all one can with brutal force and robbery.

Today there is no concern for the poor and oppressed, there is no concern for society.

May all recall these words of Psalm 33: *Blessed is the nation whose God is the Lord.*[149]

Twenty-fourth Sunday After Pentecost[150]

> *Truly, I say to you, this generation will not pass away till all of these things have been accomplished. Heaven and earth will pass away, but my words will not pass away.*
> Matthew 24:34-35

People like to reflect about the end of the world. The Revelation of God and experience based on sensible principles say

---

[149]Psalm 33: 12
[150]October 1919.

that humankind and the visible world had a beginning and so must have an end. It is only a question of what kind of end will humankind have, and when will it happen.

There are various scientific theories and views of learned persons. Lately English-language as well as Polish American newspapers have taken interest in the theories of Professor Porta who claims that the end of the world will occur this year on December 17. He bases his views on astronomical studies.

On that day the Earth will find itself between the Sun on one side and the planets and stars on the other. Devastation is to happen on Earth. Terrifying fiery masses are to burst from the Sun, magnetic hurricanes are to shake the Earth, electrical forces will fill the air, torrents of flames will reach from east to west to north to south. Frightened people will seek shelter in underground caves and great edifices but nothing will help because the Earth will not withstand the air pressure and gravitational forces, and it will either break into pieces or will fall en mass into the Sun and burn up like a little piece of coal into a great furnace.

Friends of Mr. Porta support his conclusions with citations from the Holy Scripture, which also speak of the sudden end of the world.

I will read the passage from the Gospel of St. Matthew Chapter 24. Here is the entire prophesy of Christ the Lord: *But of that day and hour no one knows, not even the angels of heaven, nor the Son, but the Father only.*[151]

If therefore no one can know about the end of the world, that in which time our globe, the Earth, will fall apart, then neither the Italian scientist Porta can know nor any of the various prophets of Protestant sects, not preachers of the Roman Church who with fear of the Last Judgment want to bind frightened simple folk forever to their Church. No! It will not be so by any means.

However, there are signs by which the coming end of the world can be known.

---

[151]Matthew 24:36.

Yes, but these signs speak to us only in general about that state of the Earth and human society in that time.

The signs are these: there will be wars, nations rising against nations, floods of blood will flow, people will be covered by streams of blood. There will be conflagrations, famine and earthquakes. This is just the beginning of the afflictions. Because after these signs the Sun will darken and through the dark expanses bursting stars will fly. Humanity will look to the future with trembling.

These are pictures of the punishment of humankind and of the uplifting of humankind.

Twenty-fifth Sunday After Pentecost [152]
The Sixth After Epiphany

The Kingdom of Heaven is like a grain of mustard seed.
Matthew 13:31

Every beginning is difficult, each work develops from a small, perfect thing and approaches higher, more perfect forms.

How small and plain was that work which Jesus Christ began.

First, as to the person of the Savior. A humble person from the town of Nazareth begins with a miraculous teaching. He was so poor that He could say about Himself: *The foxes have dens . . . but the Son of Man has nowhere to lay His head.*[153]

He works for three years in poverty with impoverished people, and His task is the creation on earth of such an order of affairs that there should be no cruelty nor sadness nor illness nor even death ...

Christ wanted to change earth into heaven. He wanted to change people into perfect holy beings. And then people threw themselves at Him and finally crucified Him.

Such was the beginning of Christ's religion, of Christ's

---

[152][1920]. Varies from year to year depending on the date of Easter.
[153]Luke 9:58.

Church.

The Kingdom of heaven is like a . . . mustard seed.

But Jesus Christ said: *All power in heaven and on earth has been given to me. And you will be witnesses.*[154] Or in other words of the Apostle, they were to accept this mustard seed and grow it into a great tree.

And they did so.

Because in them abided the power of God, the power of Christ the Lord.

Nothing encourages one to a better, noble life than a good example. Nothing awakens wonder in us like the sacrifice of one person for another.

That is why a person feels honor and love for his mother, because she sacrifices herself. Why do we feel honor for the Army? Because they sacrifice themselves. Did Christ not sacrifice Himself? He sacrificed his life for us, for our salvation.

The Kingdom of heaven is like leaven which a woman took and buried in three measures of flour.[155] What strange power is in this yeast. It changes flour, and from this flour comes bread.

Faith works similarly. Holy power flows from God into the human soul through the Word of God, through the Holy Sacraments, penance and love. As a ray of sun awakens in the soil sleeping life, a leaf spurts, a flower, so does our life awaken to a new, better life for God and neighbor under the influence of the rays of faith and God's love.

I am the bread of life. He who comes to me shall not hunger, and who believes in Me shall never thirst.[156]

If in the bread of Christ and in His religion and Church there are so many treasures and graces, and happiness, then why is humankind so unhappy?

Because it does not make proper use of God's power, God's medicine, food and drink.

---

[154]Matthew 28:18. See John 8:14-18.
[155]Matthew 13:33.
[156]John 6:35.

SEASONAL SERMONS

Sermon for the New Year[157]

Grace be to you and peace from God our Father
and from the Lord Jesus Christ.
Romans 1:7

With these words of the great Apostle I greet you at the brink of a new time. In this Christian greeting are contained all the blessings, all the wishes and all the graces which we can expect.

We have gathered here in an important moment of life. Like a lightening bolt makes the earth tremble and bursts clouds, so does this change of time thrust before us a new chance for life, and awaken us from sleep.

None of the nations neglected this change of time, even though they observed it variously. The Jews in the spring, the Romans in winter, and the Church adapted itself to this.

The Romans wanted a demigod of time with two faces: gay and young, old and troubled. During this time they drank, cavorted and had fun.

The Christians congregated in churches. And we today, imitating the first Christians, have gathered together to look back and forward and up.

1. Back. How beautiful a ship appears in port awaiting sailing. The life of a person is like a ship sailing the sea. Provided with many abilities, educated, reared by parents, one goes into the world like a ship on the full ocean of life.

Let us look back, to gather strength. First, to thank the Creator. An uncertain future awaited us a year ago; many did not survive. They were on the sea of misfortune. God supported us. So many experiences passed. The wonderful sun, the invigorating

---

[157] 1922.

101

air. So many problems, a sea of tears, so many battles had to be survived. But we managed to survive it all because God was with us. Without Him we could not have well survived the past year.

2. Yet the ship sails onward. Do fear and worry envelope us before the future? In truth, as Christians we have faith in the governance of God, and yet, when we reflect, some kind of disquiet envelopes us.

These political and social conditions. So many people died; and this is not all. New clouds are gathering. Life is uncertain and the future is uncertain for the Son of Man comes like a thief and that future may be bitter. A person deceives himself and rosy dreams often change into black reality.

A certain person compared life to a mozaic picture: every day one color, but more dark ones, more painful days than joyful ones. But if our life, our future, we place in the hands of God, then we can be sure and not fear the future.

3. A sailor sailing the sea guides himself not only with maps, not only with a compass, but also by the stars. From time to time he looks at the stars above. Sometimes on the sea storms rage and dark black clouds hide the stars. But when the storm ends, the stars come out and the ship is saved.

And a person meets trouble in life. He must look to the past, to the future and up to the star of his fate. There in the expanses of the universe is God, there is Christ the Lord, Who said: *I go to prepare a place for you . . . that where I am, there you also may be.*[158]

---

[158]John 14:3.

On the Love of Jesus Christ[159]
Sermon During a Lenten Service

I will make . . . an everlasting covenant . . in justice, goodness and love . . . so that you [the nations] shall know that I am the Lord.
Ezechiel 37:26,27

A gathering together in the name of a certain ideal always exerts a powerful and saving effect. When children gather to honor their mother and father then some strange force draws them to the family home.

To even a higher degree, it draws us to the house of God, to our Heavenly Father. We shall be gathering for three days.

What is the purpose? To remind ourselves of the goodness of God, our duties towards Him, and to strengthen love towards Him. God is love and each such gathering in the name of God is to have for its goal the coming to know this love towards Him and the One he sent, Jesus Christ.

In the Eastern language the Apostle presents this relationship as of a bridegroom with a bride: "I thee wed . . . ." Because is Christ not a bridegroom, our friend? Has He not given proof of this special love for humanity?

Love is the greatest and most wonderful emotion. We cannot give more.

You can stand before a friend and say to him: "I value you," then "I respect you, I adore you," but when you say, "I love you," you can give no more. For in this expression, "love," everything is contained.

Likewise everything is contained in this love of Christ; it includes all time and all people.

The prophet of the Old Testament, Jeremiah, said of God in respect to the Jewish nation: *With I have loved you with an*

[159]February 27, 1921. During Lent, also in Advent, Penitential Services were held for three days, usually Sunday, Monday and Tuesday. In later years they were held on Friday, Saturday and Sunday.

everlasting love . . .therefore have I drawn you to Me, *taking pity on you.*[160] Can we not adapt these words to Jesus Christ in respect to all humankind? And today Christ the Lord stands and waits. Will we push Him away and forget Him as our bridegroom and most sincere friend? He is waiting for us!

However, this Divine Bridegroom and Friend will merit our love is we take into consideration what power He came to us with and now loves us. We wonder at the person who with love for his ideal suffers. Yet who has done more for people than Christ the Lord as the Divine Messenger?

By his sacrifice one comes to know the worth of a person. Does a person who speaks of the love of God, humankind, the Church, but by his actions does not demonstrate it but does the opposite, love sincerely? No!

God first loved us, Christ the Lord loved us, of this we have proof, but do we love God?

Christ said: *Truly, whosoever believes in Me will love My word. If anyone love Me, he will keep My word.*[161]

This love is everlasting and disinterested. When people love something for someone, for the most part it is from personal interest, for a benefit, but God and Christ love us without interest for ever to the end of time.

Who shall separate us from the love of Christ, as St. Paul asks, *shall tribulation, or distress, or persecution, or hunger, or nakedness, or danger, or the sword?*

I am sure that neither death, nor life, nor angels . . . nor things present . . . nor height, nor depth . . . will be able to separate us from the love of God, which is in Christ Jesus our Lord.[162]

Nothing will tear us away nor anyone from You, our Savior!

---

[160]Jeremias 31:3.
[161]John 14:23.
[162]Romans 8:35. 38-39.

May Sermon I[163]

Once again we have awaited May, the most beautiful month of the year. The trees, the earth, the grass, are covering themselves with green and flowers, and the sun draws up new life with warmer rays.

The whole world is celebrating and in our chest the heart beats joyously. First, we rejoice that God has allowed us to await spring, and then, that as Christians we can approach in this month the Most Holy Virgin Mary and give her due adoration.

Preoccupied the whole year with matters of this world, perhaps more than one of us forgot the veneration which should surround the Mother of God. We will have an opportunity to bow our heads before her and humble our hearts and call upon her mediation and care. And we need her mediation very much. For who of us does not suffer many afflictions? Therefore in this our adversity to whom are we to turn? Between God and a person is the Most Holy Mother. As the Ark of the Covenant contained within it the law of the Old Testament and the root of Jesse, so the Mother of God brings into the world the Savior, Christ the Lord. Yet not only that she is our confidant but also our most holy healer.

Through the sins of the first people humankind lost the health of the soul, that is, the grace of God. Weak humankind became more capable of sin than of virtue, as the Apostle Paul complained: *Unhappy a man am I . . . for it is not what I wish that I do . . . I do what I do not wish.*[164]

A medicine and help for us is the Mother of God, who is our mediator, the cure of the sick and the refuge of sinners. To her we must always turn and seek her help.

---

[163] 1902. Throughout the month of May, daily devotional services were held dedicated to Mary, the Mother of Jesus.

[164] Romans 7:15-16.

The Second Sunday of May[165]
On the Cross

In the Name of the Father, the Son and the Holy Spirit.

With these words we begin each more important activity, every prayer. These words are a sign by which a Christian is distinguished from the enemies of Christ the Lord and we confess openly :

    1. That we are Christians.

    2. The mystery of the Holy Trinity and redemption.

    3. We are ourselves against all temptations.

I. In what way do we show through this that we are Christians?

We distinguish ourselves from Jews and pagans.

They recognize us everywhere by the way we behave ourselves.

We present five fingers — the five wounds of Christ the Lord.

II. The mystery of the Holy Trinity.

Hand to the forehead and in the name of the Father . . . etc. Thus is expressed the mystery of redemption.

The cross is a sign of hope.

Our help is in the name of the Lord.[166]

It shall come to pass that whoever calls upon the name of the Lord, shall be saved.[167] (St John the Evangelist, St. Benedict)

Tertulian says that Christians blessed themselves when they lay down to sleep, etc.

Cyril admonished that we should not be ashamed of the sign of the cross.

St. Augustine desires that all mothers should use this sign.

This symbol is strictly tied to the life of the Most Holy Mother.

---

[165]1902.

[166]Psalms 123:8.

[167]Acts 2:21.

Lesson on the Second Sunday of May[168]
On the Purpose of Life

The purpose of life is two-fold: closer and farther. The closer is to gain in this life relative happiness, spiritual peace, and the farther is eternal salvation.

Each person should often pose himself a question: why does he live. A child is not able to do this by itself, its parents and teachers do it for it, and usually present if the closer goal, the closer task. You live, they say, to learn, to prepare yourself for a vocation.

Such a goal is sufficient when one is a child, but when a person grows up, he must solve the mystery of life for himself.

Why do we live? In the life of Philip Neri we read about a young man.[169] And then what? He had only a closer goal. And this closer goal is worthy of efforts, work and sacrifice if it leads to the good.

One time a certain thinker visited the home of a hardworking shoemaker. The shoemaker was repairing shoes, his wife was cooking a meal, at the same time she nursed one child and another clung to her skirt. He asked: "Are you not bored?" "I am destined for this, this is the purpose of my life." And it was a closer purpose, one leading to the farther one.

Many a young man or girl leaving the family home should ask him or herself the question: Why? For what?

The biography of the Most Holy Mother says that as an underage girl she was given up from her family home to prepare herself for her future task.

---

[168]1919.
[169]St. Philip Neri (1515-1595).

The Third Sunday of May[170]
On the most important duties,
that is, knowing God and serving Him.

We all believe in one God in the Holy Trinity. Yet as thinking begins we should not only believe but we should know God in accordance with that which St. Paul said, that we should not live in the manner of unthinking animals but in the image and likeness of created beings. What then is God, is the question. The cause of all things, the Lord, etc. The pagan philosophers Socrates and Cicero believed in one God.

Where is God?

Everywhere. For how long, my brother and my sister, have you served the Lord God. From the moment when you came to use your mind.

In what was should we serve the Lord God?

In all ways, but primarily in two ways:

    1. Internal.

    2. External.

Internal: In confessing God — examination of conscience.

External: Prayer, ritual, good acts.

The First Teaching During the May Service[171]

> *A great sign appeared in heaven: a woman clothed*
> *with the sun, and the moon was under her feet, and*
> *upon her head a crown of twelve stars.*
> Revelations 12:1

As in a good family the children gather to honor their mother, since we constitute one great Christian family, we gather in this month of May to honor the Mother of God, Mary, our spiritual

---

[170]1902.

[171]May 1, 1914.

mother. Children gather and recall the virtues of their mother, her goodness, kindness, her industriousness, and with a tear in their eyes remind themselves of all the good things which they received from the hands of their dear mother.

And as we in this place will likewise consider the virtues of the Most Holy Mother, the benefits and graces gained through her, so we shall learn how to imitate, how to live in this life, that we may earn the right for ourselves to look upon her in the future life.

To gain this we must first of all determine how we are to benefit from this service, how we are to behave during this service, to experience this service, with what thought and with what spirit.

The Holy Scripture says that two people entered the Temple in Jerusalem, one a tax collector and the other a Pharisee. One apparently was just and the other a sinner. Of these two, one left justified and the other not justified. And similarly considerable numbers of people go to services, especially to May services, but how many return justified, uplifted in spirit, encouraged and worthy in the eyes of God and Mary? There are few such persons. Why? Because they do not go to church in the thought, with the intention, which God and the Most Holy Mother require.

When you pray, says the Holy Scripture, *prepare yourself so as not to be like one tempting God.* This same sentence can be fitted to a May Service. When you go to a service, prepare yourself. Do not think that his is a time to spend in socializing, a kind of stroll, but remember that this hour you should dedicate to the honor of the Most Holy Mother, that you are to spend this time closer to God and the most pure Virgin Mary. Before all, in this time we are to distance ourselves from the world in thoughts and feelings and to direct them to the Most Holy Mother. If a container is full of dirty water, then we would uselessly want to pour into it a pure fluid. So it is with us if our entire being, thoughts and feelings are directed towards the world, then will we take away any benefit from that hopeful service, from those recollections and prayers? Probably not, because the world will take up everything in our soul and there will be not room for God and the Most Holy Mother. The value of prayer depends on training, on thinking and focussing. We know this from experience. When a person rarely goes to church, he feels strange, cold, uninterested, because he does not understand the essence of prayer, but when he comes regularly, then everything affects, moves, him.

Just as a person will not benefit much by going out into the fresh air once, but when he goes more often, he benefits more.

In prayer, remembering the presence of God means a great deal. Therefore in this service there must be remembrance of God and the Most Holy Mother.

Truly her miraculous, holy form, before our earthly eyes looks like a picture, but we can see her holy soul, united with God the Father and the Son, if we will be worthy of it.

On the Love of One's Neighbor
The Feast of Brotherly Love[172]

> *You shall love your neighbor as yourself.*
> Matthew 22:39

It would seem that there is no easier commandment than the Commandment to love God and one's neighbor, but in reality a person commits the most sins against these two requirements of God.

What is the cause of this?

One of the causes is that a human being is still a little-spiritualized being. He is willful, materialistic. He cares about materials things and goals; and a materialistic person does not sense His presence.

And why do people not love a person with brotherly love.

---

[172]September 9, 1921. The Feast of Brotherly Love, a holy day established by the Polish National Catholic Church, is observed the second Sunday of September.

There are several causes. Sometimes we meet unpleasant people who are disgusting because of their superficiality and habits, who are carousers, thieves, drunkards, cynics, troublemakers, gossips, or scolds. Human nature recoils from such neighbors. A person feels a disgust which he cannot overcome.

Others, again, we cannot love because they are better than we. We feel reluctance because they are honest, just, pious, and sober.

About the year 490 before Christ, in Athens there was a very wise and noble person named Aristides. He had political enemies who decided to throw him out of his office and from the city. Aristides met a citizen who did not know how to write and who asked him to write on a tablet his name . . . .

Because he was honest and just, he went into exile.

And so today it often happens that we conduct ourselves in our love not from noble, uplifting or pious motives but often from caprice and selfishness. We love people because they are pleasant, kind, live well with us, or who look at our faults through their fingers.

Children love the kind of parents who do not punish severely errors and misdeeds, and who tolerate outbursts.

But it should be otherwise, the opposite. We should love people because that is God's Commandment. God loves all people. That He sometimes punished a person with trials, illness or death does not mean that he does not love him but He smites him to gain him. He is like one's father or mother.

What is the surest medicine for this human misery, for errors, sins, disagreement, hellish hatred, for offenses, and the weeping of unhappy humanity?

It is necessary to fulfill these two great commandments of God. The first Christians should be a model for us. We must always have in our mind and heart these words of Christ the Lord: *As you did it unto . . . even these least, you did it unto Me.*[173]

---

[173]Matthew 25:40.

The Christian Family[174]

Husbands, love your wives, just as Christ also loved the Church.
Ephesians 5:25
Bear with one another.
Colossians 3:13

Life sometimes is like a journey through a desert. The only stopping place is an oasis. This is a place in which shade trees grow, and water springs from a source. Such an oasis for a person is the family.

The family is the closest natural bond, composed of father, mother and children.

In a large sense, the family is the church, the parish, the entire Church.

Let us look at the members of the family. At the head stands the father. This is a term extremely pleasant and dear to our heart. Father — the begetter and caretaker of the family. The Holy Scripture compares the father to a magnificent oak full of branches in whose shadow a person finds family shelter. Nothing so reminds us of the presence of God as a good father, pious, noble and steady. He is the image of the strength, goodness and justice of God. Likewise, when a person wishes to honor a priest, a servant of God, he calls him — father.

The father is the image of authority, he is a guardian and friend. In good times and bad, the family comes to the father as to its most sincere friend.

The children gather around the father with inexpressible love, even though they feel honor and respect, because they know that within him beats a heart full of love and attachment. A good father thinks and dreams about the happiness of his children, and not only about material wellbeing but also spiritual. He thinks about the good upbringing and education of his son and daughter. He plays

---

[174][1921]. The Feast of the Christian Family, a holy day established by the Polish National Catholic Church, is observed the second Sunday of October.

together with his children and prays together with them.

The second member of the family, equally important as the father, is the mother. The task of the mother is to prepare the child for the struggle for life. She does this through work, love and sacrifice.

For All Saints[175]

For what will it profit a man, if he gain the whole world, but suffer the loss his own soul?
Matthew 16:26

Sometimes there are such moments in the life of a person that nothing is alluring, nothing that is light or passing. Despite one's will, serious thoughts about change, death, force themselves through a person's soul. The world presents itself somehow strange, enigmatic.

One such moment is the evening of the Feasts of All Saints and All Souls. Seemingly it is the same time, yet different. And this wind rustling through lowered branches, and these gray clouds threading across the sky, and these dried leaves, and this pale moon peering from behind the clouds — all this seriously predisposes us, and when one goes to the cemetery and looks at the cross and the graves, then despite one's will it seems to a person that some kind of voice is coming out of the earth and calling to one: *For dust you are, and into dust you shall return.*[176] And a cold shiver moves us.

Death is an important event, the most important of all. Some say that they do not fear death. . . . But two kinds of people do fear it: atheists and sinners. The atheist says that there is no immortality. Death is the most important event of all. No one will avoid the deathly breath of that terrible Angel of destruction;

---

[175][1920]. All Saints Day is observed on November 1.
[176]Genesis 3:19.

young and old, learned and simple, healthy and sick, must yield to the relentless laws of death. For what is more certain than God. And He gave the verdict that every person must die! And so we must die. About each of us someone will say: "he lived" or "she lived." Apparently healthy and strong, we bear the germ of death, because from the moment of birth death ceaselessly accompanies us.

Even the food which we consume brings us closer to the grave because in this food are rotten, spoiled particles. We consume them and contribute to our rottenness.

Uncertain is the day of our death. It is uncertain as it concerns us, but certain as it concerns God, because God marked the moment of our death from the day of conception. Death comes after us and reaches us. Suddenly, perhaps, or slowly the body stiffens and we will not be seeing God's world, nor breathing nor folding our hands in prayer.

Physical death is irrevocable, certain, although the day is not certain, but is spiritual death also foreordained by God? No! Spiritual death is our own doing. God ordained a person to happiness and salvation but gave him free will, and the person, thanks to this factor of the spirit, of this freedom, chooses sin, crime and what goes with them, spiritual death.

Here is a girl, her father a drunk and wastrel, who have gone astray. Did they not know what they were doing? They knew, because they had a choice, a free will.

Everyone is curious how our overseas Fatherland looks having arisen after 130 years of political lethargy. I came so unfortunately to Poland that I did not see either freedom or independence or unity, partly from its own fault and partly from the fault of foreigners.

Poland is free only to a certain degree. But that was to guarantee autonomy to Jews, Germans and Ruthenians.

Address on the Eve of All Souls Day[177]

And he who overcomes shall not be hurt by the second death.
Revelations 2:11

Sometimes people combine joyous and gay experiences and trials. Under the influence of cheerful music people join hands and in cavorting seek happiness . . . .

But there are times when this is not enough for a person. A person desires something more serious. Sadness and disquiet envelope him. He flees the mad tones of music, becomes more serious, and ponders the purpose of life.

What is it for? To spend life in amassing a fortune? Emptiness!

A person tries to solve the question of future life, he examines the body and the heart, the brain, goes to the cemetery, looks into the eyes of the skulls of the dead. He hears some kind of indistinct voices from the other world.

Have you ever noticed a long-distance conversation on the telephone? Similarly a person seeks a connection with another life in eternity. At first he hears indistinct voices, then ever more distinct one. To a person come the conviction that there is another, happier life. History speaks of this, the heart speaks, the conscience speaks, and Christ Jesus. *The Son of Man came to save what was lost . . . . that those who believe in Him may not perish.*[178]

---

[177]November 2, 1919. All Souls Day is observed on November 2 with prayers for the dead and the blessing of graves in the parish cemetery.
[178]Matthew 18:11: John 3:16.

At the End of the Year[179]

*For this one is foreordained for the fall
and the uprising of many in Israel.*
Luke 2:34

What a beautiful picture the holy writer unfolds before our eyes. Into forecourt of the splendid temple erected by Zorobabel, and remodeled by the elder King Herod, enters a young woman on the arm of her already graying and modestly dressed husband. To her breast the woman cuddles a baby, which she has brought as an offering to God Almighty. This mother, in whom we recognize the Most Holy Mother of God, stands among other women humbly, quietly, and waits her turn for the priestly blessing. And a wonder happens. When Mary approaches the aged priest Symeon with the Divine Child in her arms, the priest, overcome by some kind of prophetic force, takes Jesus in his hands, raises Him up and full of holy fervor cries:

Now You do dismiss your servant . . . in peace. Because my eyes have seen Your salvation, which You have prepared before all peoples. A light of revelation to the Gentiles, and a glory for Your people Israel. . . . This child is destined for the fall and the rise of many in Israel, and for a sign that shall be contradicted. And Your own soul a sword shall pierce.[180]

And these words will come true to the iota in the passage of twenty centuries. Christ the Lord was for some everything, God, Savior, the good shepherd, the best benefactor; for other people scoffed at, ridiculed and forgotten.

And for you, Brothers, who did Christ become in the course of this unhappy year in this parish? Did Christ become happiness and salvation — or perhaps destruction?

---

[179]1905. A crisis occurred in the Polish National Catholic parish in Plymouth, Pennsylvania, in 1905 with the departure of the pastor, Father Joseph [Józef] Dawidowski from the Church, when the congregation divided.
[180]Luke 2:29-32. 34-35.

I did not think that it would come upon me to speak to you from this place because people of a foreign faith wrote that a priest, whom I sent here as a guardian of the National Church, as a guardian of the Most Holy Mother, the Queen of our Nation and Patroness of this church, is giving up the care of this church to another faith and dares even to draw along the parish.

Others again of our unfortunate brothers in hotheadedness and greed cried that they will sell this House of God built to the glory of the Most Holy Mother and turn it into a public hall.

Anger and contrariness wanted to triumph over the people's work, suffering and National ideals. Yet behold that the spirit of God blew and the Tempter stopped in all his ugliness and they rejected him, and only a handful of reprobates remained. For this God deserves thanks today.

And also for other benefits received from Your hands during the course of the past year, Lord. We stand at the brink of the old and the new year. A few thoughts.

We believe that everything comes from the generosity of God. Each good thought, every excellent word, each noble deed, and every breath of a person and the smallest insect, are governed by and fulfilled according to holy laws. But in an especial way we thank You, Christ, that You did not abandon us in this year but took care of Your people.

You said to the Apostles when You were to pass from this earth to the Father: *But I will not . . . forsake you . . . . I will not leave you orphans, but will remain with you for all days to the end of the world.* [181]

Therefore Christ remained through the Word of God proclaimed in every church, He remained in the Most Blessed Sacrament, he remained with all who followed in his footsteps, for he said that if anyone loves Him and keeps His teaching, then He will come to him and abide in his soul and heart.

And we give thanks to God this day for a piece of bread in a

---

[181]Hebrews 13:5: John 14:18.

foreign land. In toil and labor it must be won. It is true that we were not hungry, neither were your children nor wives.

And there in the wide world, what is happening? The newspapers inform us that in India alone about eighteen million people died from hunger, and from various illnesses such as plague, cholera and leprosy another million human beings closed their eyes forever. How many groans, pain and grief! And here in this land we were saved from that.

And we also have to thank the Lord for what is happening in our Polish land. Truly, hunger threatens there too, except for that, the virtues of our nation have improved.

INDEX